Broken Bones May Joy

Studies in Reconciliation and Resurrection

ALAN WEBSTER

Warden of Lincoln Theological College

But thou wilt sin and grief destroy;
That so the broken bones may joy,
And tune together in a well-set song
    Full of his praises
    Who dead men raises
Fractures well cured make us more strong.
George Herbert

SCM PRESS LTD

LONDON

To
Alison, John,
Stephen and Catherine

SBN 334 00144 7

First published 1968
by SCM Press Ltd
56 Bloomsbury Street London

© SCM Press Ltd 1968

Printed in Great Britain by
Quicks the Printers, Clacton-on-Sea, Essex

CONTENTS

CONTENTS

PREFACE

INSIDE the walls two hundred prisoners in drab, badly fitting grey, with a few warders at the corners of the ground, were standing on the touchline watching a game of soccer between the prison and a team of ordinands. Obviously a lot of tobacco was at stake. 'Up the Vicars', 'Up the Mission' were answered by 'Up the Reds', 'Up the Nick'; or even, by a very respectable elderly prisoner beside me, 'Up the Residents'. It was all very clean, and gentlemanly. The referee was a prisoner, using the padre's borrowed watch, and if he had a bias it was towards the theological college. I gathered that the public stake was an extra film on Sunday, so I was glad that the prison won 4–2. I gathered, too, that the prison team had agreed in the padre's room that language, at any rate on the prison side, was to be limited to Damn, Blast and Bloody.

It was the first time an outside team had played in the prison and I was glad that Christ's twentieth century disciples had had the idea. Even so the men standing around, with greyness going deeper than their clothing, shut up because this is the best that we can do, threatened to fill one with despair, though the excitement of the game and the tough parson-rotting jokes of the spectators now and then broke through the gloom with a sharp jab. At least that game was better than doing nothing about the alienation between prisoners and the outside world and I felt it revealed some penetration of the greyness of prison life with Christ's spirit. When Nietzsche said that 'His disciples should look more redeemed', he was rightly protesting against a pale grey Christianity which is false to its founder and will never commit itself to the struggle for new life in a new, re-created world.

This incident at the prison led me to ask whether reconciliation is not at the heart of the Christian life and to write this small book for Lent and Easter 1968 to explore ways in which the task of reconciliation is being carried out today. Anyone who has had the good fortune to work for friendly north country parishes in Sheffield and Durham, as well as for those lively intelligent communities called theological colleges, has seen that men and women and children are still enlisting in the service of reconciliation.

I should like to thank my colleagues and other members of the college for their help, the Reverend David Edwards for inviting me to write this book, Mrs Wray for typing the script, and my wife for many suggestions and much encouragement. I also owe a debt of gratitude to David and Pam Wilcox in whose ever-open home in South India the proofs were read.

ALAN WEBSTER

1

FORGIVENESS FEELS LIKE DEATH

In his war novel, *Iron in the Soul*, Jean-Paul Sartre caricatured the happy character who could see no difficulty about forgiveness. His motto was 'Not to grin is a sin' and his temperament 'overflows with love for humanity in general, children, birds and abstract painting'. He believed that the 'only thing needed to settle all conflicts was a little common sense'.[1]

Any investigation of forgiveness must begin with a recognition of its difficulty. Though we have been taught to forgive minor and even major injuries naturally and easily, no one finds it simple to bury the hatchet and not to make a virtue of burying it, still less to refrain from marking the place in the ground. If the conflict has involved anything we really care about, forgiveness will be costly. Yet because so much effort has been put into training us to forgive, to be tolerant and conciliatory and to look for compromises and agreement, we can easily forget this cost and be blithely self-righteous about those who do not forgive others, and dangerously censorious of ourselves, when we suddenly experience the real price of forgiveness. It is not man's métier to forgive.

William Blake's remark that 'Every act of kindness is a little death' sounds exaggerated, especially on a sunny day when we are not living calculated lives considering each moment from our own point of view. But to forgive may mean that one is prepared to sacrifice one's rights, to tear a piece out of oneself, to take the risk of offering all this only to see it rejected as a relationship of love and instead grabbed as of right, with no understanding whatever of the cost involved. There is always the danger of

[1] J.-P. Sartre, *Iron in the Soul*, H. Hamilton (1948); Penguin ed., (1967) pp. 1–15.

suffering the anguish of seeing that those one cares for and loves do not want what one has to offer.

The cost of forgiveness comes not only from the danger of rejection but from a sense of mortgaging the future. Forgiveness often appears to be simply dealing with a past debt, but it always implies the creation of a new relationship which will affect the life one is going to live. Forgiveness is always directed towards the future. What is past cannot be undone, but the future is open. For example, 1870, 1914 and 1939 can never be erased from German and French history, but reconciliation for these two countries means a new, costly relationship in which neither country can be totally independent.

To forgive is to let go of one's control over one's own destiny. If I forgive the thief, how do I know that he will not return, thinking me weak and easy-going? If I forgive the man who takes away my reputation, how do I know that he will not return and take away my life? To forgive is to do battle with one's whole determination to stay alive and assert oneself, it is to surrender the power of self-direction. To surrender one's self-control, even under the anaesthetic of the trusted surgeon, can be difficult. To surrender it to the man who has injured one can feel like suicide. Again and again this tension between self-preservation and the duty to forgive has been ignored. We think that forgiveness ought to be easy, and this in turn has exacted the extra penalty which has always to be paid when human affairs are based on illusion.

In practice, communities and individuals find forgiveness a perennial problem with which all the increased resources of human knowledge, psychological, sociological and technical, continue to struggle. The difficulty of forgiveness on the grand scale in the twentieth century has been more obvious in our colossal world-wide wars succeeded by periods of peace and rearmament. There is no easy deliverance for any community whatever its degree of commitment to the Christian outlook; Britain used force at Suez, the United States over Vietnam; and India, where the Gandhian way of non-violent resistance had most support, was compelled to fight on its own frontiers. 'The snare is broken, and we are delivered' cannot be securely claimed by any nation if the deliverance is from fear, from revenge, from the tragic shrinking from mutual acceptance. Again and again it has looked as though not to resist but to accept and forgive the aggressor would be the death of the forgiving community.

Forgiveness is made no easier when we realize that self-awareness is the beginning of advance towards God. When we say 'I cannot forgive myself' or when we think 'If only I had been given a different temperament' or 'If only I had not made that decision', we are facing the problem of self-forgiveness. Still more difficult does forgiveness become if we are aware of the divided self with all the complexities and anxieties this involves. Here the psychiatrist is often as baffled as the apostle whose anguish about himself arises from the difficulty of self-acceptance. 'I do not understand my own actions. For I do not do what I want, but I do the very thing I hate. . . . I can will what is right, but I cannot do it. . . . For I delight in the law of God, in my inmost self, but I see in my members another law at war with the law of my mind. . . . Wretched man that I am!' (Rom. 7. 15–24). St Paul's words might be a transcript from a psychiatrist's notebook on contemporary self-disillusion. Self-awareness and an understanding of our mixed motivations will prevent us from being cocksure, but it will not immediately move us to the awkward step of actually forgiving.

To turn to the Bible for clues about reconciliation is to discover an approach which accepts the real difficulty of reconciliation. In the Old Testament, the Law and the Prophets stress both the will of the righteous and holy God who must be obeyed at all costs and the sinfulness of all mankind who are his children and for whom he cares. Again and again we are introduced to prophets who thunder and moralize and condemn and we sense that they are standing for vital truths without which humanity would have been impoverished and Israel would have been as forgotten as the Hittites. The God whom we discover is not slack and genial, pliant and obliging, but a God who is holy himself and requires holiness, justice and truth from those who would serve him. It is made very clear that it does matter how we live – it matters eternally. Amongst the harsh angular facts of life, the wars of petty kingdoms, the struggles between the rich and the poor, the arguments of the purveyors of new ideas and the defenders of traditional ones, the true servant of Yahweh is to do justly and love mercy and walk humbly with his God. Forgiveness in the Old Testament is represented as a struggle; Yahweh struggling with his prophets and, it seems, even sometimes with himself.

The words most commonly used in the Old Testament for forgiveness, and the atonement which leads to forgiveness, are all metaphors for dealing with sin. It is covered, put behind God's back so that it no longer stands in the way of a free exchange of love. Or it is carried away, so that the road is open. Or it is forgiven so that there is no resentment poisoning the relationship, or anger which prevents a fresh approach.

Is there any condition for forgiveness? It is usually said that in both the Old and the New Testaments the condition is repentance. You must first repent and then you will be forgiven. But this is an inadequate view of the depth of understanding which is typical of the Bible. Repentance is emphasized but not as a direct cause of forgiveness, as though forgiveness could be automatically ensured. What is insisted upon is our own forgiveness of those who have hurt us. As William Temple pointed out, 'Only one petition in the Lord's Prayer has any condition attached to it: it is the petition for forgiveness. . . . Our plea is to rest on our attitude, not towards God, but towards His other children. He is always ready and eager to forgive; but how can He restore us to the freedom and intimacy of the family life if there are other members of the family to whom we refuse to be friendly?'[2]

The idea of covering or atoning for sin is the source of what became a Christian proverb summarizing the divine attitude which is to be characteristic of the disciples of Christ: 'Love covers a multitude of sins' (1 Peter 4.8). A strong determined love goes on forgiving until seventy times seven, in other words, without limit.

In his *Works of Love* Søren Kierkegaard analysed this saying and grappled with the problem of the shutting of the eyes to reality which the saying raises.

[2] William Temple, *Personal Religion and the Life of Fellowship*, Longmans (1926), p. 46.

It is easy to see that the lover who discovers nothing looks very mediocre in the eyes of the world. . . . And this is the curious thing: if someone had discovered how fundamentally humane almost every man is, he would scarcely dare to make his discovery known for fear of being laughed at. . . . That which the world admires as shrewdness is an understanding of evil; wisdom is essentially the understanding of the good. . . . Blessed the believer, he believes what he cannot see; blessed the lover, he believes that sin away which he still can see. . . . But why is forgiveness so rare? Is it not because faith in the power of forgiveness is so little and so rare? . . . But when love forgives, the miracle of faith takes place.[3]

Christ's vivid vignette of the Pharisee and the Publican praying side by side in the Temple showed the religiously correct representative of Judaism in contrast with the man who simply threw himself without qualification on God's mercy, as if he was instinctively turning to someone who would accept and understand and forgive. The Publican's patriotism, honesty and religious discipline were probably slack but he went away justified and forgiven, whereas the Pharisee was frustrated and left the Temple despising his neighbour.

It would be unfair to draw the conclusion that Judaism did not understand forgiveness. The religion described in the Old Testament shows a growing sense of a people convinced that they were in personal relationship to God who favoured them and fathered them and made demands upon them, who was angry and sorry and jealous and righteous and holy, and again and again, when faced by his unsatisfactory people, proved to be forgiving. Yahweh is the very opposite of the everlasting, unchanging God of the philosophers, drained of passion, imperturbable and unmoved. He was experienced by Israel as a God who cared and forgave because he was concerned with people, whose character was gracious, full of loving-kindness and tender mercy.

The Old Testament is long and complex, but again and again we find that the men we meet share with us a continued concern with persons and the need to treat persons with sensitive understanding. This is the moral of that moment of truth when Nathan the prophet, confronting David, who had sacrificed

[3] R. Bretall, *A Kierkegaard Anthology*, OUP (1947), pp. 318–320, 418–425.

Uriah to his own desires and had mercilessly contrived his liquidation in battle, told his story of the ewe lamb, so inducing David to condemn himself. The unmerciful David felt himself convicted as immoral: the prophet's words scarcely needed the 'Thus saith the Lord', for they were self-authenticating. David simply knew that they were true (II Sam. 12.1–25).

The words of a recent Bampton Lecturer in another connection are a valid comment on this incident: 'People who refuse a proper concern for persons are immoral as human beings and wrong as judges of matters of fact.'[4]

We can trace a growth in the Old Testament stories of the conviction that the God of Israel was forgiving and that his servants must themselves be forgiving. When David felt the callousness of his treatment of Uriah he said, 'I have sinned against the Lord', not 'I have sinned against Uriah'. The greatest of all the psalms on the theme of forgiveness, Psalm 51, 'Have mercy on me, O God', describes sin as an offence against God and the prayer for forgiveness and renewal is made to God.

Jeremiah was able to speak of his own experiences more openly than any other personality in the Old Testament and no one saw more clearly that the new covenant or relationship which Yahweh was creating would be intimate, in the heart of each believer, and would give each person the ability to respond with free and open joy to God's love. The blocks of guilt and sin would be removed by the gracious personal forgiveness of God: 'I will forgive their iniquity and I will remember their sin no more' (Jer. 31.34). Thanks to Jeremiah's own self-awareness and his ability to understand God's way with him, he discovered what God hoped to do with every one of his people – namely to forgive them, to renew them and to restore them. His conviction was that God was at work in the heart, in the depths of his personality, and that there could be personal communion with God and that this inward link was real because God forgave sins.

The straightforward directness of this way of thinking of God's determination to forgive is magnificently stated in the assurance of the final verses which conclude the Book of Micah,

4 David E. Jenkins, *The Glory of Man*, SCM Press (1967), p. 3.

where the divine concern to forgive people is seen as a proof of his power:

> Who is a God like thee, pardoning iniquity
>   and passing over transgression
>   for the remnant of his inheritance?
> He does not retain his anger for ever
>   because he delights in steadfast love.
> He will again have compassion upon us,
> He will tread our iniquities under foot.
> Thou wilt cast all our sins
>   into the depths of the sea (Micah 7.18, 19).

In the Cross and Resurrection of Christ the first Christians knew that these prophecies had been fulfilled and that they had ample power to meet whatever came with fortitude, patience and joy.

> He rescued us from the domain of darkness and brought us away into the kingdom of his dear Son, in whom our release is secured and our sins forgiven. He is the image of the invisible God; his is the primacy over all created things. . . . Through him God chose to reconcile the whole universe to himself, making peace through the shedding of his blood upon the cross – to reconcile all things, whether on earth or in heaven, through him alone. Formerly you were yourselves estranged from God; you were his enemies in heart and mind, and your deeds were evil. But now by Christ's death in his body of flesh and blood God has reconciled you to himself. . . . (Col. 1.13–22 NEB).

In the New Testament the cross is not simply the scene of Christ's sufferings, the occasion where most is to be forgiven because an innocent man is suffering unjustly at the hands of church, state and people; it is the centre of God's self-giving. Whereas for Jews at certain periods death had been seen as the final defeat, the grim horror, so that it was obvious that a living dog is better than a dead lion, for all Christians at all times the cross becomes the very centre of God's reconciling work. Through an evil so ugly that we are not sure whether children ought to look at pictures of it, God finds a way to us – in the death of Jesus Christ.

To acknowledge the reconciliation effected in the death of Jesus Christ does not mean that we can wholly grasp how God worked. God grasps us and we do not grasp him or his ways. The cross keeps us open to the conviction that even when man

13

as a matter of fact did the worst that he could possibly do to the Son of God, namely reject and kill him, God found a way of forgiving and reconciling. In this mysterious discovery that in unmerited suffering there is another dimension which leaves open a way to a new freedom, lies much of the 'newness' of the New Testament.

Dr John Knox, writing on the link between the Cross and the Christian life, has said:

> Accepting the Cross does not mean understanding it; it means almost the contrary – recognizing a dimension and a potency in human life which defy our comprehension and all our little systems, whether of law or truth. It means also recognizing, again without understanding, that God's love is somehow able to manifest itself in and through suffering as in no other way; that the evil in human life, which . . . constitutes the decisive argument against God's reality, also gives God his supreme opportunity to manifest his reality. . . . How does it happen that we cannot witness another suffering unjustly, but in love, without feeling that somehow he is suffering for us?[5]

The Cross, then, is for the New Testament the centre of God's active forgiveness, which is not passive or unadventurous or even a state of endurance as though the forgiving man was a brave but beaten boxer who takes all that comes and staggers on to be saved by the bell. 'Forgive', like *pardonner* and *vergeben*, is a strengthened form of the word 'give', as though this was giving to the power of *n*, in fact until seventy times seven.

Christ the reconciler has been described both as the lamb of God that takes away the sin of the world, offering his blood as a sacrifice, and as Christus Victor who defeats the demonic powers which would destroy the relationship between God and man. These are not easy ways of thinking about Christ's reconciling work today, but they point so clearly to the heart of the problem and are so deeply woven into Christian thought and worship that they need to be understood rather than abandoned. But those who find this language difficult deserve an answer. I remember an undergraduate saying, 'I can't believe a religion which speaks about the sacrifice of Jesus Christ. It's so crude; it sounds like cannibalism when you speak about drinking his blood in the service of Holy Communion.'

[5] John Knox, *The Death of Christ*, Collins (1959), pp. 170–1.

The offering of blood is a Jewish sacrificial concept. In Jewish sacrifices it was the ritual with the blood of sacrificial victims that was regarded as the crucial sacrificial act that brought about atonement, the re-establishment of proper relations between God and man. The Epistle to the Hebrews, arguing that sins could never be removed by the blood of bulls and goats, re-interpreted sacrifice as the offering of the will. ' "I have come to do thy will. . . ." It is by the will of God that we have been consecrated, through the offering of the body of Jesus Christ once and for all' (Heb. 10. 4–10 NEB). The author saw the death of Christ as a free, personal, voluntary gift to act as a bridge to restore relations across the gap of alienation.

We may reinterpret some of the thought of this epistle in Dr Forsyth's fine words:

> When we speak of the blood of Christ we mean that he drew on the very citadel of his personality and involved his total self. . . . His whole personality was put into his work and identified with it. . . . The saving work of Christ drew blood from Christ as it drew Christ from God – and not from God's side only but from His heart.[6]

George Herbert and the Wesleys in their poems on the Cross of Christ tried to spell out the link between the passion and pains of Christ and the love of God and to see them re-presented in the Eucharist. In Herbert's words:

> Love is that liquor sweet and most divine
> Which my God feels as blood; but I, as wine.

Wesley used the same language:

> O that our faith may never move,
> But stand unshaken as thy love!
> Sure evidence of things unseen,
> Now let it pass the years between,
> And view thee bleeding on the tree,
> My God, who dies for me, for me.

The phrase 'forgiveness through the blood of Christ' insists crudely, almost brutally, on the cost of Christ's reconciling work for men.

Blood also points to the struggle involved, the battle which has to be fought whenever the odds against forgiveness are

[6] P. T. Forsyth, *The Cruciality of the Cross*, Independent Press (1948), p. 93.

15

high. In the Old Testament this was often emphasized by speaking of the anger of a jealous God, which means not the irrational outburst of passion (as if God was an oriental despot or a Greek deity of uncertain character) but the consistent determination to combat sin and evil. Such anger can be seen in the New Testament in Christ's conflict with unworthy conceptions of God set out in the five stories of conflict in St Mark, chs. 2–3.6. The description of Christ as a pale Galilean does no justice either to the prophetic, creative figure of the gospels or to the risen Christ who is the Lord of the Church today.

It is right to see that the blood of Christ, in P. T. Forsyth's words:

> expresses not simply the bleeding of the feet that seek the sinner but the bloodshed of the battle that destroys the prince of this world . . . and establishes the holy kingdom.

The righting of any great wrong involves this same costly pouring out of blood in the toils and aches of a Wilberforce or a Livingstone. Bonhoeffer put this same truth for us when he wrote to Reinhold Niebuhr describing why he must return from the safety of America to the grim dangers of Germany:

> I must live through this difficult period of our national history with the Christian people of Germany. I have no right to participate in the reconstruction of Christian life in Germany after the war if I do not share the trials of this time with my people . . .[7]

Bonhoeffer rebelled against cowardly apathy which could never reconcile his German people with the true and righteous God. Faith in Christ is again and again a faith which will rebel and whose sign will be written in blood. Until a Christian has run some real risk for Christ, even if it is only the risk of ridicule or failure, he has not become a disciple. In his service only wounded soldiers can serve.

Sometimes the young see this more clearly than the elderly and settled. Dr Cyril Alington used to tell the story of a boy who was discontented with a picture of St George and the Dragon in which St George was driving his spear home for all he was worth but had no wounds, not a scratch. 'It looks a bit too easy,' said the boy. 'My idea of St George isn't quite so

[7] Quoted by Reinhold Niebuhr, 'The Death of a Martyr', *Christianity and Crisis*, Vol. 5 (June 25th, 1945), p. 6.

16

spick and span . . . any sort of wounds would do, but if you ask me, I should have thought he might have had them in hands, feet and side – and some marks on his forehead where the thorns had pierced. . . .'

It is not only the theologians and the preachers who have described Christ as Lamb of God and as Christus Victor, as the leader in a great struggle against the dark forces of death and sin and disease. Artists and poets have again and again caught this mood of the victory of forgiveness. The triumphant star-surrounded crosses in some of the ancient buildings in Ravenna speak primarily of the victory of forgiveness. One of Wesley's finest hymns to be sung at the Eucharist is in the same mood:

> Hosannah in the highest
> To our exalted Saviour
>> Who left behind
>> For all mankind
> These tokens of his favour:
>
> His bleeding love and mercy,
> His all-redeeming passion
>> Who here displays
>> And gives the grace
> Which brings us our salvation.
>
> Louder than gathered waters
> Or bursting peals of thunder
>> We lift our voice
>> And speak our joys
> And shout our loving wonder.
>
> Shout all our elder Brethren
> While we record the story
>> Of him that came
>> And suffered shame
> To carry us to glory.

I believe that all Christians have experienced these moments of joy in the triumph of Christus Victor when there has been a reconciliation we could not reasonably expect. Perhaps – against what seemed all the probabilities – a marriage has come to life again, or a friendship which seemed finally broken has been restored, or a Christian community bound by its principles not to accept a Roman Catholic or a Protestant has suddenly opened its fellowship to the stranger, or a teenager comes out of a self-destructive wilderness of drugs – then we do want to shout our loving wonder and we know as a matter of fact and not as a theological theory that our Lord is Christus Victor, seeing in our own experience that broken bones may joy.

But we cannot forget the other fact of the Lamb sacrificed and suffering that takes away the sin of the world. We have all seen this story relived – in tired, red-eyed men sweating to separate the cars locked in tangled destruction on the bypass through speed or carelessness or just drink; or perhaps in the family of the overworked general practitioner in hospital with thrombosis at forty-five because the Health Service has made unlimited demands on a conscientious and courageous man; or the solicitor working without a partner and finding time for voluntary work as well. Perhaps we have seen this story relived in the woman who looks after her family and manages to be the person who 'copes' when the neighbours need her or her church looks for someone who is gay and totally reliable to give a touch of stability to the young people's club. Whenever we see this we can thank God that his love is still being poured into human hearts, even when God is working so anonymously that he is not recognized.

The result of the whole history which the Bible describes, in both the Old Testament and the New, was the creation of a people who felt free to proclaim the Gospel to anyone who would listen, whatever their nationality or background, whatever their way of life and whatever the cost of the proclamation might be. The Gospel was felt to go to the heart of human life and to be able to surmount the barriers and frustrations just because at the heart of the Gospel was the universal experience of death. The claim of faith was that in the death, in the Cross itself, God was at work and that in the Cross and in the Resurrection it could be seen that God was in Christ, reconciling the world to himself. The first Christians were those who resolved to live in the light of the conviction that God had done something absolutely unique in Jesus Christ and that this made a difference to their whole way of living.

2

RECONCILER UNLIMITED

THE basic belief which controls the Church's worship and its way of living is that God became man in order that man might become like God. The purpose of the divine experiment was reconciliation, the reconciliation of God and man and of man as he is with man as he ought to be. This central Christian conviction leads, its adherents believe, to an authentic way of life which is not unnatural because it is God's way; the supernatural is the supremely natural. Christ's words, 'Father, forgive them for they know not what they do', as he was being crucified and finally giving up his life, reveal man at his most glorious as well as God at his most forgiving.

The Christian account of forgiveness reaches its climax in the story of the Cross and Resurrection, when God's forgiving love was seen in its fullness in one man. In all ages men have looked for love and feared loneliness and revered those who could enlarge their capacity for love. Now this unending search for love was over, for Jesus Christ had been uniquely generous and uniquely self-giving. Perhaps he did not go to his death deliberately intending to give his life for the sins of the world, but in his death he revealed God's care for men, the love that moves the sun and the other stars.

To be a member of the Church, so the New Testament insists, is to share this conquering and suffering love of Christ. There are no other rules and all the creeds and canons and conditions are secondary, sometimes helpful, sometimes not. That God was in Christ reconciling must never be understood by the Christian only as a historical statement of what happened nineteen hundred years ago. In an era of change as rapid as we know now men will soon cease to be interested in what happened nineteen hundred years ago – unless it is actually true of lives today. A style of living, a way of looking at life, and not accounts in books alone, not even in the Bible, will convince others of the truth of Jesus Christ.

All the New Testament writings are attempts to describe this reconciling approach to life. 'If any man would come after me, let him deny himself and take up his cross and follow me' (Mark 8.34) and 'Whoever does not bear his own cross and come after me, cannot be my disciple' (Luke 14.27). Reconciliation is to come even before formal religious duties. 'If, when you are bringing your gift to the altar you suddenly remember that your brother has a grievance against you, leave your gift where it is before the altar. First go and make your peace with your brother, and only then come back and offer your gift' (Matt. 5.23, 24, NEB). Christ's remark about forgiveness to seventy times seven, which we have already quoted, is a warning that to be reconcilers we may have to give up our desire to do a quick job, perhaps to satisfy our ego or our impatience, in order to devote ourselves to the slow development of a personal relationship which will finally bridge the gap.

But did Jesus Christ as a matter of fact stand for unlimited reconciliation, either in his teaching or his conduct? We are told that when no one would answer his question, 'Is it permitted to do good or to do evil on the Sabbath, to save life or to kill?' he looked at them with anger and sorrow at their obstinate stupidity' (Mark 3.4, 5 NEB). The struggle against the dark powers of lovelessness stirred him deeply because he felt that the hardness of their hearts prevented them from recognizing God's gracious work in him. Reconciliation is a struggle and those who resist have to be fought.

As an agent of reconciliation Jesus could be almost brutally savage and direct, as Pasolini in his film masterpiece, 'The Gospel according to St Matthew', makes so clear. Jesus was a passionately realistic leader, knowing men's capacity for defending the indefensible if their own systems or interests are threatened. In the heat of this kind of battle we do not find a calm serene Jesus keeping his emotions and his temper rigidly under control, as some of the ways in which the doctrine of the sinlessness of Christ has been presented suggested that he did. Christ was not afraid of controversy.

In the accounts of Christ's fierce arguments with 'the Jews' in the Fourth Gospel, especially in chapters 8, 9 and 10, we are told that because they sit in judgement on the Lord and misinterpret his words they will die in their sin. In St Mark, and more especially in St Matthew, the Pharisees and Sadducees are bitterly denounced. Even if allowance is made for the writers being influenced by later Jewish hostility to the Christian Church, the pictures are of such intense controversy that liberal and fair-minded Jewish scholars have concluded that had Jesus loved his enemies he would not have called them vipers, or predicted their arrival in hell.

It is fair to point out that what Jesus was denouncing was the hypocrisy and exclusiveness of the Pharisees, but we may wish that more accounts had survived, including some from the point of view of the Pharisees. We need more information than we possess if we are to do justice to Jesus and the Pharisees. Possibly this is one of those moments when we see that Jesus found his own teaching and convictions about forgiveness, which he vindicated wholly on the cross, hard to practise when faced by skilful opponents. 'He was tempted at all points as we are, yet without sin.' His vocation was to be a reconciling person, but this was a hard vocation which ultimately cost him his life.

But the image of Christ which lives is not that of the controversialist but of a man whose inner life was one of unique love for others. 'Having loved his own . . . he loved them to the end' and 'This is my commandment, that you love one another as I have loved you' (John 13.1; 15.12). Christians have felt that the love of the risen unseen Christ is richer and deeper and more inclusive even than the records actually say – that his reconciling love is beyond the powers of the evangelists, who could do no more than point to an ineffable, unlimited reconciling love in Christ.

Of course it is dangerous to say that we know more about Christ than what the gospels explicitly tell us. We can start creating fictions of our own imagination, making Christ sugary and sentimental or liberal and this-worldly, to name two perils

21

of modernizing Jesus in the twentieth century. But 'we have this treasure in earthen vessels' and the Jesus Christ who reconciled us by his death and is with us through his resurrection will always be beyond us. The gospel accounts are not BBC news bulletins but were written that we might believe, that through this faith we might possess eternal life.

Jesus certainly struck his contemporary critics as scandalously generous over forgiveness. The friend of publicans and sinners, the Son of Man who claimed power to forgive sins, even on the Sabbath, the man who was prepared to single out the Samaritans for praise despite all their irregularities, seemed to be dangerously permissive. But his permissiveness was always for the sake of others and not for the sake of an irresponsible easy life for himself. His basic principle that God is a loving father involved the corollary that all men are his children and that active care, concern and goodwill are required from every one of us. Christ's greatest interpreters put this very strongly. 'If I bestow all my goods to feed the poor but have not love, it profiteth me nothing' (I Cor. 13.3). 'If a man say, I love God, and hateth his brother, he is a liar' (I John 4.20).

The parables of the Lost Sheep, the Lost Coin, the Prodigal Son and the Great Feast are all designed to drive home the fact that God is endlessly generous and that forgiveness is a free gift – to those who will turn to God and away from self-justification, and show a forgiving spirit to others. 'And whenever you stand praying, forgive if you have anything against anyone; so that your Father also who is in heaven may forgive you your trespasses' (Mark 11.25).

Two of Christ's beatitudes are especially revealing about forgiveness. 'Blessed are the merciful for they shall obtain mercy' strikes home to Christians who must often confess the strain of harshness which so many authors and artists have seen as disfiguring the Church, which brought Christianity to Peru with the methods portrayed in *The Royal Hunt of the Sun*,[1] or which inspired the way of life described in *The Barretts of Wimpole Street*[2] or in *A Woman of the Pharisees*.[3] This hard, unimaginative

[1] P. Shaffer, H. Hamilton (1965).
[2] R. Besier, Gollancz (1930).
[3] F. Mauriac, Eyre & Spottiswood (1946).

22

attitude of mind can still condemn the unmarried mother and her child or the newly released prisoner as though Christ had not spoken. In fact he wished his followers to show kindness in action, to be prepared to renounce their pride in respectability and to have the faith which rebelled against lovelessness, the faith so splendidly lived whether in a St Vincent de Paul, a Mary Slessor of Calabar or a Trevor Huddleston, or in so many unknown social workers.

'Blessed are the peacemakers for they shall be called sons of God' gives the same blessing to active reconcilers. It is strikingly translated in the French *Bible de Jerusalem* as 'Les artisans de paix', which suggests the hard slogging of a Dag Hammarskjöld slowly building up an international civil service, teaching men to live with provisional arrangements, with his bags always packed ready to go wherever he was needed. The emphasis is on peace *making*, and Christ was drawing on the Old Testament understanding of the need to fight for and create peace as described by Isaiah: 'For to us a child is born, to us a son is given; and the government shall be upon his shoulder . . . of the increase of his government and of peace there will be no end. . . to establish it, and to uphold it with justice and with righteous-ness' (Isa. 9.6, 7). These are the practical virtues of the statesman and the administrator who has to live with the consequences of his decisions.

Mercy and peace are understood as dynamic, demanding, and to be striven for. 'Never pay back evil for evil. . . . If possible, so far as it lies with you, live at peace with all men. . . . Do not let evil conquer you, but use good to defeat evil' (Rom. 12.17–21). The note of judgement which Christ sounded so strongly in his allegory of the sheep and the goats at the great assize and in the story of the older brother at the end of the parable of the prodigal son is directed against those who are complacent about sin and injustice and do not make the effort to be peace-makers, militants for forgiveness.

The Sermon on the Mount carries the lesson of these beatitudes even further when we are told to turn the other cheek and to love our enemies and not on any account to retaliate. This seems to take us into a fairy-tale world and away from the real world of competition and the rat race and the need to stand up for ourselves. Helmut Thielicke, speaking in Germany just after the war when the land was crowded with refugees struggling for living space in the countryside and cooking facilities in the kitchens of the tenement houses, described these commands as the most difficult in the New Testament. And yet we have to learn to treat the possibly slovenly, demanding refugee as the brother of Jesus Christ with the royal courtesy of love. Not retaliation, but a new set of values, is the command which can make a bridge into the neighbour's and even into the enemy's heart.[4]

Participation in the reconciling work means, according to the New Testament, not only being willing to forgive, but watching for the opportunity and seriously reckoning with the possibility of a fresh start, a resurrection, whatever the circumstances. The Christian is to be so awake, so principled without being ponderous, that he can help the world in which he finds himself to more human relationships and ways of living. The repeated 'Watch and pray' of the Lord in the gospels, the impression one gets of Christ really listening and being available, the artist's observant eye which created the parables about forgiveness, are all essential to the divine work of reconciliation. In Christ we can see a sympathetic, respectful attitude to others based on the conviction that love will lead to reconciliation and joy.

Christ's followers have not always managed to make his spirit their spirit by being alert in their forgiveness. Charles Williams wrote that 'some Christians make a burden of things which non-Christians would pass over lightly. They overdo forgiveness as they overdo patience and other virtues.'[5]

Often we need encouragement at precisely the right moment. Those who did pioneering work for the unclubbable, as described in Mary Morse's *The Unattached*,[6] found that at times their work was almost unbearable because of the isolation and the difference between their fundamental values and the 'bum' philosophy of some of the teenage groups. There was a danger

[4] See H. Thielicke, *Life Can Begin Again*, James Clarke (1966).
[5] Quoted by C. F. Evans, *The Lord's Prayer*, S.P.C.K. (1963), p. 160, from *He Came Down from Heaven* and *The Forgiveness of Sins*.
[6] Penguin Books (1965).

either of cynicism about the whole project or of a critical and judgmental attitude towards the people they were trying to serve. Only the encouragement of an experienced supervisor, who could act as a catalyst and prevent their attitudes so hardening or weakening that responsible relationships could not be maintained, enabled these isolated, and to some extent anonymous, workers to carry on. One of them said afterwards:

> Under the considerable pressure of the last drama production, I grew rather tired. My ability to control my feelings was not as strong as it ought to be and I found myself increasingly affected emotionally by the whole activity. At one point, for example, I was very sharp and impatient. . . . I became very resentful. . . . The onus once again seemed to be left to me and, somewhat irrationally, I showed my annoyance. . . .[7]

The New Testament imperative of 'Watch and pray' is a warning that even when we are doing the work of reconciliation, natural and inevitable feelings aroused by being ignored or laughed at need a safety valve, which may be provided by a colleague who understands our frustrations. Anyone who has tried to control a difficult club late in the evening knows how easily normal friendliness can be destroyed and anger and despair take charge.

In their understanding of the Good News the first Christians knew that they had experienced *metanoia*, a turning of the mind, so that they now faced God and had been baptized for the forgiveness of sin. They knew that they were reconciled and were in Christ and that death and sin had no power over them. But they soon discovered that, despite this divine forgiveness and reconciliation, temptation was not over and that every kind of actual sin had eventually to be dealt with inside the church.

This was a shock which had to be faced very early, when the Epistles were being written. We can see it clearly when the younger Pliny, who was Roman governor in Bithynia in 112 A.D., wrote to the Emperor Trajan to ask for his advice in the treatment of Christians. When he began to examine the Christians an anonymous pamphlet was published by an informer containing a great many names. When some of these people were

[7] ibid., pp. 199–200.

questioned they said they had been Christians but had recanted three or even twenty years before. We can imagine how difficult for the church was the problem of what should be done with those who denied Christ as well as with those who failed in other ways. Gradually and reluctantly a system of confession and absolution, first public and then private, was evolved.

Further changes in attitude followed the acceptance of Christianity as the official religion of the Roman empire. Whereas baptism had meant the dramatic and dangerous acceptance of a new life with an assurance that the sins of the past were forgiven, now the normal citizen was baptized, probably in infancy, and the sense of reconciliation and of belonging to a reconciling church was weakened. A thousand years later it seemed to some of the Reformers that they had been brought up to believe that forgiveness had to be earned by attendance at the sacraments and was the final goal of the Christian life rather than its origin and spring as it had been to St Paul. Luther and other reformers were the revolutionaries who insisted that man is always a forgiven sinner whose relationship to God depends upon what God has done for him on the Cross and not on his puny efforts at self-improvement and religious growth.

The Christian today who confesses his sins either privately in a service or in his own prayers or with a priest in confession or in counselling, is heir both to the New Testament and Reformed understanding that we are forgiven sinners and to the understanding of the Church that we shall need help with our particular sins and the assurance that God has forgiven us, if we are to be reconcilers ourselves. The aim of confession will always be the strengthening of the relationship with God rather than an analysis of sins of omission or commission, so that by release from guilt and remorse we can be more open to God and each other.

This may be a way of knowing God, knowing each other, and knowing ourselves and of discovering that neither God nor the priest or pastor or friend or even our own conscience is primarily a judge. Here is a way we can deal with our shyness, pride, and that feeling which is so common in this country, of not wishing to be beholden to anyone. If we remain buttoned and bottled up, shut up in ourselves, we cannot breathe the atmosphere of reconciliation.

Personal counselling, making one's confession, the trusting and challenging conversation of the small group, of course arise from different needs, but they share at least one aim, to breathe this atmosphere of reconciliation and mutual trust and love. They ought not to be regarded only as group techniques – all are sacraments of friendship and reconciliation, all are moments when we may encounter both each other and God in a deeper personal relationship and go away the stronger and the braver for it. We all need much more encouragement to go further into friendship with others and with God – the relationship we call prayer.

One of the discoveries the Church is making today is its need to be more creative if it is to be open to the reconciling love of God and able to be a base for reconciliation itself. The days of Christendom, when the official leaders of the Church could muster their forces and proclaim a truce of God or even mobilize the committees which pushed through the anti-slavery legislation, are over. When the work of acceptance and forgiveness has to be done for particular groups, such as those despairing of life or those involved in marriage difficulties or education in the under-developed countries, new societies – the Marriage Guidance Council or the Telephone Samaritans or Voluntary Service Overseas – must be formed. More and more flexibility will be needed if the Church is to function effectively as a base for reconciliation in an increasingly diversified society.

But whatever organizations the Church encourages, its essential task in reconciliation will always be to bring the crucified and risen Christ before men, including those who do not explicitly belong to the Church. One of these, Dag Hammarskjöld, in his *Markings*, was constantly returning to the theme of divine reconciliation as the one hope of the future, the way in which we say 'yes' to our neighbour and to destiny:

Jesus' lack of moral principles. He sat at meat with publicans and sinners, he consorted with harlots. Did he do this to obtain their votes or did he think he could convert them by such 'appeasement'? Or was his humanity rich and deep enough to make contact even in them, with that in human nature which is common to all men, indestructible, and upon which the future has to be built? . . . So shall the world be created each morning anew, *forgiven* – in Thee, by Thee.[8]

Christ's work as reconciler is unique because of his complete devotion to God's will to bring reconciliation, and his complete understanding of the way in which everyone is dependent upon each other – an understanding, humanly speaking, derived from the centuries-old experience and reflection of Judaism. As one of the most perceptive of all modern theologians, Baron von Hügel, wrote to his niece: 'I wonder whether you realize a deep, great fact? That souls – all human souls – are deeply interconnected. That we cannot only pray for each other, but *suffer* for each other.'[9] Christ staked his life on this fact.

Christ, the reconciler, knew anger and frustration, he experienced anxiety at many levels, the everyday anxiety of disciples bickering about sincerity or worrying about housekeeping, the much more searing anxiety of his mother suffering in his suffering, and the deepest of all anxieties, the fear that there is no meaning and no purpose and no one who cares, which he expressed in his cry from the darkness of the cross, 'My God, my God, why hast thou forsaken me?'. He knew from his own experience what it means to feel that nobody minds, that there is no reservoir of concern and caring in the world. He was

> a man of sorrows, and acquainted with grief;
> and as one from whom men hide their faces
> he was despised, and we esteemed him not.
> Surely he has borne our griefs
>   and carried our sorrows (Isa. 53.3, 4).

Historians, sociologists, psychologists and others are gradually discovering the mechanism of human solidarity which was intuitively perceived by Judaism, Christianity and other religions long ago. This solidarity need not imply the brute force or, worse still, the hidden persuasion of massed numbers, but it can be the means through which we recognize each other as members of a single family, all drawing on the same store of divine con-

[8] D. Hammarskjöld, *Markings*, Faber (1964), pp. 134, 138.
[9] D. V. Steere (ed.), *Spiritual Counsels and Letters of Baron von Hügel*, Darton, Longman and Todd (1959), p. 22.

cern. As more and more is known about the mechanism of the relations between men, the personal decisions, whether to love, whether to forgive, whether to care, whether to be tolerant and to listen, become more and more important. The very inter-relatedness of modern technology increases the power of any small group, which press their own interests unreasonably, to cause immense dislocation but also increases the opportunities for realizing that we live together in one world.

Redemption, atonement, even reconciliation, sound remote and 'theologically' complex words to use to understand, for instance, those who work in a great teaching hospital where community can be seen at its most skilled and devoted, and yet where anxieties about status or the special traditions and rights of the surgeons, doctors, nurses, administrators and technicians can cause friction among the staff and unhappiness among the patients. But these are not only parallels with the ideas expressed in these old Christian concepts; they are describing the same processes of understanding, the same common store of caring and the heavy blocks which so often impede co-operation. In the hospitals, as in so many large-scale modern concerns, the understanding that everyone from the surgeon to the cleaner is involved in each other's hopes and fears, failures and successes, triumphs again and again. The sensible, everyday dictum that he who stands on his dignity will be left standing, puts the point pithily and hints at deeper truths about human co-opera-tion.

' "But to convince you that the Son of Man has the right on earth to forgive sins" – he turned to the paralysed man – "I say to you, stand up, take up your bed, and go home" ' (Mark 2.10). A supreme sign that God was at work among men in his own chosen one was seen in the extraordinary powers of release which Christ was able to use, release from sin, from guilt and from sickness. At the centre of the Christian faith is the conviction that the divine will to forgive is still at work through the risen Christ in the Spirit.

3

RECONCILIATION
IN THE INDUSTRIAL WORLD

RECONCILIATION is at the heart of the Gospel because the Gospel is concerned with the deepest human needs. It is true that some manage to live without asking fundamental questions about the meaning of life or apparently feeling any tension between what we hope to be and what we actually are. Some men appear to avoid the struggles which divide men at work, or men at prayer, or men divided by nationality. They believe we shall be able to build a tolerant, pluralist, secular and cosmopolitan society where reconciliation is unnecessary, for harmony is assured.

Much of this ideal Christians would want to share, but they would question whether there is any inevitability about progress to this goal. If we actually look at men at work, at men in the churches and in their national groups, the Gospel's concern with forgiveness seems more realistic. When we have glanced at these three needs we shall try to see with the poet's eye before considering the Eucharist as the means of reconciliation. We begin with reconciliation of man at work and must first face the question as to whether the Gospel has anything to say.

The sentence was one hundred years' hard labour after a verdict of 'mainly guilty'. This was the surprising conclusion of a group Bible study in South India at which the church was tried for disbelieving that the Gospel had any relationship with social justice. Among the witnesses who were called were Amos and Isaiah: Amos gave evidence in no uncertain terms about the people of God in his day in Samaria about 760 BC: 'I will not revoke the punishment; because they sell the righteous for silver, and the needy for a pair of shoes – they that trample the head of the poor into the dust of the earth, and turn aside the way of the afflicted' (Amos 2.6, 7). As an oppressed minority the early Church had less to say about the just ordering of society than either the prophets or the contemporary Church, but the social implications of the Gospel and Christian teaching about the nature of man were not forgotten. For modern Christians these consequences are crucial, as the lives of Wilberforce, Shaftesbury, Livingstone, Gladstone, Schweitzer, R. H. Tawney, William Temple, Kagawa, Martin Luther King and so many others testify. But for them the sentence would have been doubled.

In the past the conscience of Christians has led them to press for reforms. Dr Stafford Clark has instanced Mr Samuel Tuke, the Quaker, whose family founded the Retreat at York after revealing to the public the appalling conditions at the York Asylum. The groups which pioneered Christian Aid and Oxfam, in which Christians and non-Christians have joined, have revealed some of the hideous hunger of the underdeveloped countries.

In England today social justice and the productivity of industry are inter-related problems, which dominate every election and all political discussions. Though most people have a basic interest in the quality of the work which they are doing, this interest is reduced by the feeling that workers are employed by the management but led by the unions, and so involved in a tug of war between the two in which loyalty requires support of the unions. The worker is often aware that the union group-solidarity, in which he is involved, may be working against his interests as a consumer or house purchaser, that strikes lose him money and that higher wages may mean higher prices; he may rely on the government of the day to control or influence the union of which he is a member. Within the works, however, his emotional loyalty is to the union and the union's *raison d'être* is to withstand the management, which even today sometimes remains harsh and privileged. The memory of the depression of the 'twenties and 'thirties and the more distant memory of Peterloo and the savage struggles of the bleak age of the early nineteenth century still lives and is revived whenever there is recession and redundancy.

How can the Christian concern for conditions of work and genuine co-operation in meeting human need be expressed today? Naturally it is already the concern of Christians working in industry, of Christian politicians, whether Conservative, Liberal or Labour, and that small group of theologians who follow in the steps of Reinhold Niebuhr and William Temple, who insisted that Christian belief had social consequences. It is the concern of the industrial missions now being created in so many cities in Europe and America. It ought also to be the concern of all parishes, all dioceses, and above all of the men training for the ministry. After all, as Hans-Ruedi Weber, of the Department on the Laity of the World Council of Churches, has so well said: 'The laity are not the helpers of the clergy so that the clergy can do their job, but the clergy are the helpers of the whole people of God, so that the laity can be the Church.'[1]

The gap between the men in the factory and the church is seen at its sharpest in the gap between the clergy and industry. In the country and in the country towns the clergy have been involved in the schools and local affairs and have made it their business to be around in the markets and on the farms. But in the cities it has been rare for clergy to visit the factories, offices and shops, and if they have done so they have often felt themselves to be out of place or have been taken round and wined and dined by top management. This divorce has led to a failure to think hard enough about industrial life, so that human values and welfare have been sacrificed too easily to industrial productivity. Possibly this is a hangover from the days when going into business was regarded as of a lower social status than working for one of the professions. Certainly Christian thinkers have done far more work on the ethical problems of war, personal morality and colour than on economic and industrial questions.

Today the gap between the ordained ministry and the factory work is so wide that only men with great patience and no show-manship can bridge it. Ecclesiastical authorities, Roman and Anglican, are often inept and heavy-handed – witness the fate of the priest workmen in France and the difficulties of the

[1] Quoted by J. A. T. Robinson, *The New Reformation?*, SCM Press (1965), p. 55.

Sheffield Industrial Mission in Britain, after they had been founded by pioneering bishops, such as Cardinal Suhard of Paris and Leslie Hunter of Sheffield. But where ministers will work in a friendly humane way, with the explicit backing of the management and the men, expressed through the trades union, a new atmosphere can be created. The chaplain becomes a man who wins trust because he has been around in the works week after week over the years. To spend a day in a Lincoln factory with an industrial chaplain, who was himself an engineer before he was ordained, and to experience the straightforward open relationship, entirely human and unforced, which has been built up over the years, is to experience the beginning of recon-ciliation. Of course in Lincoln the gap is not so great as in other cities; the man on the test bed for the diesel engines may be a bell-ringer on Sundays, even if he goes to the pub rather than to service when he has finished ringing. One of the trades union officials belongs to the local church and has a view about the sermons and thinks that the unions are like the churches – both have a large *nominal* membership. Another official is clearly a man who believes that persons matter and, though he belongs to no church, can recognize other people who believe with him that the personal in life is basic. So he can see the chaplain to be a friend and frequently an ally.

All chaplains are likely to be involved in the misunderstandings which face any reconciler. Should they become involved in works politics as did Henri Perrin, the great French priest workman, shortly before his tragic death? Should they encourage men to ask questions about noisy or dirty conditions of work? Should they support the management when men fail to use the safety guards which are provided? What should be the chaplain's attitude to such abuses as ruthlessness in the rat race or petty pilfering? These are real questions for all English works chap-lains, and there will be cases when the chaplain must stick his neck out, just as there will be occasions when he must defend the 'official' church to which he belongs. Most of the time, however, he will be a catalyst rather than a critic; just by being in the factory and becoming part of it he will quietly remind all who happen to see him or to speak to him of something we all easily forget – the Gospel and its promise and its values. He will have to think and to challenge, so that in his conversations in the works and the discussions which may take place outside, changes in attitude may occur. The chaplain becomes a catalyst whenever he is able to help men to see each other as fellow human-beings who are bound up in the bundle of life together.

Two trades unionists who had sat silent during a long discussion in a meeting in a theological college on divisions in industry, were finally prodded on to their feet. One got up and, referring to some remarks by the new managing director, said, 'This is just fairy-tale language. We can't believe our ears. Mr X (the managing director) would never say what he has just said anywhere where it mattered.' Mr X at once replied that he had meant every word he had said and that he was prepared to say it all again when actually negotiating. In fact Mr X is one of those managers who will find time to listen and who is felt by the men to be involved in their good and the good of the firm: the chaplain had found a way in which those common interests would be appreciated.

The German minister, Horst Symanowski, who has been committed to this kind of ministry in Mainz-Kastel, writing of the service of Christians to man in the secular world, has rightly said that our purpose is not to set up a

> 'Christian society' alongside the worldly social order so that Christians may dwell happily among themselves divorced from the world, but rather, to help the secular society to find its way to more human relationships and forms of organization.[2]

The first step must be to find ways in which the Christian ministry is not only exercised on Sundays at altar and pulpit, but goes outside the walls of the church and reminds us of God and his claims in our work and working relationships, where we are often very different persons from what we are at home. Reconciliation is in the office and the factory and not simply in the home, as the emphasis which the Church has put on the home has often suggested.

The ministry of managers and employers is naturally far more

[2] H. Symanowski, *The Christian Witness in an Industrial Society*, Collins (1966), p. 169.

influential than that of factory chaplains, even if the factory chaplaincy system were extended as it ought to be. A coal board manager who has to close redundant pits can cause immense hardship to families as well as to pitmen. If he takes trouble to see every man, to organize work not too far away, to plan the closures gradually, to listen to representations, his work will be much more complex and demanding, but he will be acting as a humane man with a real concern for human welfare. (How unfortunate it is that 'welfare' is often misunderstood be limited to to the provision of canteens and sports clubs!) If he goes further and makes provisions for removal grants and refurnishing grants, he is showing that he understands what it means for a man's family to be moved in the interests of greater production. All this is involved in being an agent of reconciliation, and one does not have to go far to find managers who are doing this, both in nationalized and in private industry.

The great pioneers of reconciliation between the workers and the church have found that being a witness, often simply listening, working alongside others, being with rather than mainly preaching or organizing, is extraordinarily costly. It may mean living where you would not choose to live and perhaps bringing up your family where you would not choose to do so. It may mean receiving very little sympathy from your church, as the heroic French Jesuit, Henri Perrin, discovered when he became a worker priest and began to represent the workers in their disputes with the management.

Horst Symanowski wrote: 'But let's have no illusions about this: this is dangerous business! . . . Being a neighbour cost Jesus his life. Will we get off any cheaper?'[3] Symanowski works for reconciliation by insisting that, in the mutual conversation and concern for each other in modern industrial society, God is at work. The Church can be reborn if Christians can learn to listen and to be alongside, qualities far more important than the old symbols of church buildings, bells, steeples and pulpits.

One example of how some men training for the ministry faced this challenge in practice may contain hints for parishes and other Christian groups. It is a worm's eye view of conditions in steel

[3] ibid, p. 55.

works, but it has implications for industrial society which are far wider.

This particular plan was evolved partly because I was only too aware of how inadequate my own training had been to equip me to go as a curate to Attercliffe, an east end parish in Sheffield of 50,000 people, with some of the largest steel works in the country. Apart from working on a farm and in forestry camps, the only work I knew was at school and at university. But the boys in the Sheffield club it was my duty to run (we met in a broken-down pub called 'The Licensed Victualler', with the former landlord and his wife usually in bed in the front room) were all at work, mainly in steel. One day I was taken by Ted Wickham, now Bishop of Middleton, to Samuel Fox's Stocksbridge works and made to stand on an empty oil drum in front of a group of men beside a furnace to answer their questions about the Church and whether it was a good thing that parsons should come into factories. Fortunately they believed that the Church should look after young people and approved of youth clubs, and gave me an easy run.

My own nervousness on that oil drum made me a strong supporter of the much more realistic training now given to men who are to work as priests in industrial areas. For instance, every year since 1961 ordination candidates from Lincoln, with men from Wells, Westcott and Cuddesdon occasionally joining in, have taken part in courses sponsored by the Scunthorpe Industrial Mission and various Scunthorpe steel works, especially the Appleby Frodingham Steel Company and Richard Thomas and Baldwin (Redbourne Section). The students on these courses, which have each lasted at least six weeks, have produced reports which have been based on their work and afterwards hammered out in discussion with management and union representatives. No one would expect startling discoveries from men who worked for no more than a month or so in the labour pool before starting their investigations, but the fact that they were independent, that they were men of good will and that there was no hint of patronage or the giving of good advice from outside, made these reports valuable to the works concerned as well as to the ordinands. One works manager, well known for his bluntness as well as his efficiency, remarked when a report was being assessed: 'They've done a damn good job: I wish some of them would leave the Church and come into steel.'

One or two details from these reports pinpoint some problems in industry which are so vital and yet so hard to solve. The project brief for the 1961 course, which like all the briefs was determined by the firm, was entitled 'Communications at Work'.

Our problem is to convey accurately information to work people about the many things which concern them. . . . By studying the works' problem in communications, it may well be that the students will be assisted in the Church's own problem in communicating with industry.

The project teams were restricted to studying the written communications, including those of the Safety Department. Their method was to work out questionnaires which were usually answered verbally and were checked as often as possible by conversation. The method was not elaborate; any group of men and women given the good will of all concerned could do as much.

One problem of communication through the firm's magazine which rapidly emerged was the question of syrup or emetic, 'Do we prefer a rosy picture or blood and tears, toil and sweat?' Do men respond better to a diet of good news, progress and the stress on the firm as a 'happy family' or to articles entitled 'How daft can you get?' Of course an article directed against an individual would smack of victimization, but when a General Works Manager published over his own signature articles attacking those who spread false rumours and those who so overloaded a wagon with nearly 48 tons of ingots that it was derailed, 91 per cent of those questioned approved of the articles. (It is only fair to add that the platelayers, far from being chastened by the warning of the overloaded wagon, were thrilled that their department should have been mentioned in the works' newspaper at all!) The shop floor much prefers to be given the real facts and is far too shrewd to be taken in by a false image. There is a cartoon stuck up in one of the cabins in this Scunthorpe works – the boss is talking to his men across a desk: the caption reads,

'This firm is one big happy family and it's got to stop'. A rosy picture which avoids all mention of possible short time and of the absolute need to sell the product, creates a feeling of unreality and being treated as children.

The safety both of the workers and the product has been the subject of laws and regulations since Lord Shaftesbury and others attacked conditions in factories and mines. Both at Scunthorpe and at Detroit there have been investigations of safety precautions and the attitudes of management and men towards them. Naturally Scunthorpe and Detroit firms do their best to foster a sense of accident awareness and no one comes to work with any other intention but to go home whole, but steel-making is dangerous the world over. The safety regulations are threatened by such common attitudes as 'It can't happen to me', 'I'm all right, Jack', 'Safety is a finicky detail', 'Safety-guards reduce output and so affect piece-work rates'.

In the bad old days of the early industrial revolution safety regulations were resisted on the ground that nothing must be allowed to increase the price of the product. In the great nineteenth century debate on safety in the mines, especially children's safety, William Cobbett remarked that it used to be asserted that Britain's greatness was due to her navy or banking system. 'Now,' he added, 'it is admitted that our great stay and bulwark is to be found in 30,000 little girls. . . . Yes, for it is asserted that if these girls worked two hours a day less our manufacturing greatness would depart from us.'[4]

The recent reports of the Scunthorpe courses have dealt with the urgent problems for British industry today – productivity, mobility and the best use of human resources. They form a commentary on the Statement of Intent on Productivity, Prices and Incomes which the representatives of management and unions undertook on behalf of their numbers in 1965: 'To encourage and to lead a sustained attack on the obstacles to efficiency, whether on the part of the management or of workers, and to strive for the adoption of more rigorous standards of

[4] Quoted in *Shaftesbury and the Working Children*. Documents edited by J. Langdon-Davies, Jackdaw Series, No. 7, Jonathan Cape (1964).

performance at all levels.' Questions such as 'Why is productivity in Britain comparing unfavourably with that in other steel-making countries?', 'Why does some labour become too mobile, so that, like a boulder on a hillside, once work-people have been induced to move it is difficult to keep them?', and 'How can school children be given a true picture of the opportunities in a steel works?' are not only questions for experts but may concern every citizen. These are questions to which it is difficult to give answers and which point to problems which can only be coped with if society itself is well informed. The old paternalistic notions that all that is needed are clear orders, and that joint consultation means joint notification, are no longer accepted.

Working in the general labour gang at a Scunthorpe steel works, perhaps alongside Pakistanis who spoke little English and found laying railway tracks in the snow a grim job, soon revealed the complexity of work as it is in practice. 'The business of a steel company is to make steel and not to provide good human relations,' says the 'realistic' commentator, but even the labour gang, who are the lowest paid workers, matter for the well-being of a steel works. In the experience of the students, manning of jobs can be haphazard: 'When you want six men concreting you get two, and when you only want two you will get six.' 'In the Labour Gang more time is lost through the tacit assumption that every job will take a multiple of seven and a half man hours (i.e. one man's whole working day) to complete, than through any other single cause.' Men who complete a job in good time are transferred to sweeping, often so aimless that they cannot clearly see the purpose of the work. So Professor Parkinson's satirical law that 'Work expands to fill the time available for its performance' is found to be true. No one admits to being underworked but morale is lowered when un-necessary work is required – the sweeping up of coke and coal spillages from conveyor belts, tracks and strips, which are in-efficiently planned and maintained. The active unionists who assert that 'there is no bad labour – only badly organized labour' have some powerful arguments. The fear of redundancy from deflation, from cheaper steel from abroad or from the introduction of new machinery, is real, and cannot be met by accusations of Luddism. A steel-worker has little status or seniority outside his industry or even his own works if he is dismissed. Reversion to labouring is usually as great a fear as drop in wages.

It is this fear which maintains the legalistic demarcation disputes. Yes, let's do away with these stupid barriers – provided of course you do not affect my livelihood and my status. So skilled men in the engineering section of a steel works may have to leave one job they are on and cross the plant simply in order to do something for another skilled man of a different craft who is waiting for them to arrive, though he was entirely capable of doing the job himself. Demarcation disputes can spread a malaise of delay and nonsense, which can affect the entire engineering services. A clearer understanding of the need for close co-operation by thousands of men for the production of steel, a greater trust that society will not desert redundant workers, and a greater interest in the work itself are all needed if reason not fear is to settle the demarcation disputes.

Good communications within factories are important: it is as important that there should be good communications with the rest of society. Scunthorpe is far-sighted, the reports reveal, in creating many kinds of links. Relations with local schools, recruitment of men slowly returning to normal life after mental illness, the courses for theological students, are all evidence of a healthy openness. The reports suggest that more could be done to integrate the industry and the schools by talks from those actually engaged in steel-making, so that young men joining the works may know what they are doing. This will help towards solving one of the major problems – the turnover of 20 per cent per annum in those who work for the firm. How can men joining a vast modern factory with 10,000 workers feel part of a team, each man growing in self-confidence as a steel worker, with increasing confidence in his firm? Much depends on those in charge of new workers and whether any personal contact is made by the foreman. The manual worker, especially the recently recruited manual worker, needs to be made to feel he is important to the company: a good induction course helps here, and the major distinction in many firms between staff and manual workers has the reverse effect. The Marlow Declaration, a little noticed Christian effort to improve the atmosphere in British industry, has well said:

> The most valuable asset of a company or other organization is manpower, not in financial terms, nor in capital equipment, but in the skill, knowledge, loyalty, enthusiasm and goodwill of the people which it employs and with which it does business.[5]

A study in 1966 in one large steel works indicated a steady increase in the instability of the labour force over the previous three years, not only in the labour pool, which is always changing, but among older men who have been with the company for years. 1,207 men left in 1962/63, 1,392 in 1963/64 and 1,781 in 1964/65 (an increase of 28 per cent over 1962/63) without any appreciable change in the total number of men employed. With the full co-operation of the union a careful questionnaire was circulated to discover what could be done to help men to feel fulfilled in their work. There was no one answer. Short-time working in steel reduces wages and security; younger men especially dislike shift working; promotion, particularly for maintenance men, is difficult to organize; and training and retraining is not sufficiently expert. In many respects the British steel industry has been an example to other industries in its labour relations and there have been few strikes since the war, but there is still room for improvement in meeting the human needs of the workers.

The reports of those young men working for two months in the steel industry are refreshingly non-judgmental. In the past, Christian leaders have been too ready to pronounce verdicts. The attitude of Archbishop Randall Davidson in 1926 at the time of the General Strike was a most honourable exception. At the cost of being prohibited from broadcasting by the BBC, which was, as Professor Asa Briggs has shown in his history of British Broadcasting,[6] in danger of being taken over by the government (Churchill's group were pressing for this), the Archbishop insisted that both sides to the dispute had a case

[5] *The Marlow Declaration, III*, 3. This Declaration, published in 1963, stressed the need for greater acceptance of responsibility by the individual for society. It is discussed in *Crucible*, July 1963 issue.

[6] Asa Briggs, *History of Broadcasting in the United Kingdom*, 2 vols. Oxford (1961, 1965).

and so, in the words of a non-Christian humanist, became the conscience of the nation. Too often the Christian voice has been that of the outsider, unintentionally harsh. Dr Hensley Henson's splendid qualities of courage and independence are seen at their worst in his attitude to social problems, even in County Durham itself, where he was so critical of the miners collectively and so devoted to them as individuals. If he could have put himself amongst the Jarrow hunger marchers as he had sided with the workers in the Putamayo atrocities, his eloquence and powers of leadership might have been used to the full instead of being frittered away in arguments about the 1928 Prayer Book. Before, and even occasionally after the war, the parable of the Labourers in the Market Place was still expounded in the pulpit as a condemnation of workers who wanted to increase their wages, rather than as a parable of the unstinted grace of God.

Much more needs to be done at many levels if the Church is to be an informed reconciler within the nation, aiding solutions of the major political problems, including relationships and productivity in industry. Parishes could spend far more time in studying social and industrial problems, since fortunately there is a mass of recently published material to help them, including Denys Munby's *God and the Rich Society*,[7] Daniel Jenkins' *Equality and Excellence*,[8] the synopsis of the reports of the Church and Society Conference of the World Council of Churches at Geneva, entitled *Christians in a New World*,[9] and several Christian Education Movement study outlines.

The Industrial Missions, which are now to be found in places as diverse as Coventry, Chichester, Corby and Crewe, are uniquely qualified to assist parishes, chapels, Christian groups and theological colleges to develop a more alert concern for doing the will of God in the industrial world. Perhaps the day will come when the cathedrals with their staffs and chapter houses will become centres of reconciliation and dialogue. Though the Methodist Church at Luton has been in many ways a pioneer, a special responsibility for national welfare in the broadest

7 Oxford (1961).
8 SCM Press (1961).
9 ed. D. L. Edwards, SCM Press (1966).

sense rests with the established church. Its traditional concern for the nation lays upon all its members, lay and clerical, the urgent task of bringing together the Gospel and industry.

Some parishes already have great experience in committing the congregation or groups within the congregation to intelligent and determined action. Holy Trinity, Dalston, in North London, led the local opposition to the Fascist anti-Semitic meetings in Ridley Road and is now deeply involved in the struggle to integrate immigrants. To attend the parish communion with a white and black choir and congregation along with a lively young group from the nearby Congregationalist Church in Dalston, is to get a glimpse of the unity without uniformity for which we hope in the future. In Sheffield, Holy Trinity, Darnall, has been holding parish meetings ever since 1941 on a pattern previously used in Frizington in Cumberland, and once again there has been a wholehearted committal of the church to the claims of social justice, the rights of the unemployed, of Pakistanis in Sheffield, and to political involvement over many problems. No one will forget the friendliness, openness, controversy and chairmanship of the Darnall parish meetings.

It is a mistake for parishes or Christian groups to think that they can whip themselves up about social justice for some special occasion, a general election or some specially controversial question such as Suez. Unless there is the conviction that the Gospel is always relevant to social justice, and that the crisis is one more event about which we must think and decide in the light of our conscience, a special meeting or a controversial sermon may be a gimmick. But at present the churches are still too withdrawn. During the 1965 General Election, a survey of the Lincoln churches and chapels was carried out to discover how far sermons, prayers, or meetings referred in any way to the election. The results showed that, though the Free Churches were rather more involved than the Church of England, the general attitude was that above all the churches must be neutral. This was carried so far in one or two cases that there were protests because the Lincoln Council of Churches held a public meeting at which both Labour and Conservative candidates spoke, on the ground that politics were best avoided by Christians. In fact the meeting itself, which was better attended than many local political meetings, discussed Rhodesia, Vietnam, educational and economic policies fully and fairly.

Would it be possible for parishes or youth clubs, especially in large cities, to carry out a survey of some particular social need? Working out the questions and getting them answered can stir the sleepy and awake the complacent. Though the Church is no longer the Conservative Party at prayer, it must not be allowed to become the Neutral Party at rest. Sometimes a small frontier group of laymen drawn from a number of parishes can work effectively, especially if using the magazine *Frontier* as part of their agenda. There can be a surprising welcome for the gospel of reconciliation when it can be recognized as concerned to bring peace through the breaking down of all walls of hostility.

4

RECONCILIATION AMONG THE NATIONS

THE reconciliation of the nations is one of the dreams of the Christian faith. 'When nation shall speak peace unto nation' is one of the marks of the new age, a sign that God's Kingdom has come. Then every nation, tribe, people and language can unite with one common aim, one common life and one common worship.

For this grand consummation the Church is intended to be a preliminary model on a small scale. Sometimes we can see this happening today, as in the North London parish already referred to, with its mixed black and white choir and congregation; or in ecumenical conferences where all the nations, eastern and western, make their distinctive witness to the Gospel. Sometimes we can see this in a parish meeting – I think of one in Sheffield – where different nationalities come and it is not all sweetness, but the repressed antagonisms can be expressed and discussed.

When the Church fails to be the place of reconciliation and loses sight of its supra-national vocation, the failure is always felt as a deep betrayal of its inner spirit. The English churches, which since the war have found it so intolerably difficult to welcome the West Indians, most of whom were churchgoers before they emigrated, or the churches of the United States, which kept their schools and worship segregated, have felt a growing sense of guilt. Churches which are not places of reconciliation are not true to their real selves.

Jesus Christ's approach to the reconciliation of the nations is surprising. He confined his own personal ministry and that of his disciples to the tiny country of Palestine; from Dan to Beersheba is roughly the distance from Northampton to

Southampton. He questioned the proselytizing activities of the Jews round the Mediterranean world, and in his own encounters with the Gentile Syro-Phoenician woman (Matt. 8.5–13) and the Gentile centurion (Mark 7.24–30) made it clear, before he granted their requests for healing, that his mission was to Israel.

But at the same time he was a skilful opponent of all pretentious nationalism and ideas of revenge. Though he had at least one Zealot among his disciples he went out of his way to emphasize the virtues of the Samaritans and Romans. He healed a Samaritan leper, his story of the Good Samaritan was designed to shame his fellow countrymen, and when he was told of the dreadful massacre of Galileans by the legionaries he apparently made no comment on the Romans but saw the sinister event as a call to Israel to repent (Luke 13.1–5). He also warned Israel that at the final judgment their place might be taken from them by the Gentiles. His parable of the Kingdom of God as a king's feast to which the obvious guests refused to come and which could only be filled by men from the highways and hedges, gave a new place not only to the fringe outcasts of Israel but also to the Gentiles.

Very soon after the Resurrection, however, Christ's disciples knew that they must go into all the world and that they had a special secret mission 'to hold the world in unity'. The Epistle to the Ephesians described this as 'breaking down the middle wall of partition' and 'summing up all things in Christ'. Two or three centuries later the *Epistle to Diognetus* outlined this hidden work of unification in these words:

Christians are not to be distinguished from other men by country, language or customs. They have no cities of their own, they use no peculiar dialect, and they practise no extraordinary way of life. Residing in cities of the Greek world and beyond it, as is the lot of each, they follow the local customs in clothing, diet and general manner of life, but at the same time they exhibit the constitution of their own commonwealth as something quite paradoxical. They reside in their own homelands – but as aliens. Every foreign land is home to them, every homeland a place of exile. In a word, what the soul is in the body, Christians are in the world. The soul is dispersed through all the members of the body, and so are Christians among the cities of the world. The soul is enclosed in the body, but holds the body together, and Christians are enclosed in the world as in a prison, but it is they who hold the world in unity.[1]

Today we would not describe the world as a prison, but we are aware that if Christians are wholly absorbed by the culture in which they live they cannot be salt or yeast. The calling of the Church is to be a nucleus, aware of its faith and united in its worship, so influencing the nation around it that many who do not explicitly describe themselves as Christians accept Christ and his values as the supreme picture of what they believe ought to be true and what at their best they would like to be.

Part of the task of this nucleus committed to reconciliation is the proclamation in all seasons, friendly or harsh, that ultimate authority rests not with the earthly state nor even with some vast multi-national organization such as Rome or a future United States of the World, but with God himself. This is not a theoretical assertion but one which insists that there are no specially righteous or specially hypocritical nations; all tend to pursue nationalist policies for their own advantage and all need to acknowledge a law or a standard above them. The old symbol of the cross and orb surmounting the crown, pointing to the subordination of the earthly state to the *Civitas Dei*, must not be asserted to put 'Christian' nations on a higher level than 'non-Christian' nations but to put all nations under scrutiny.

Reconciliation between nations is always costly and cannot be achieved by surface politeness and easygoing accommodation, not because nations are inherently immoral but because they are powerful and demand that justice shall be done to their being as nations. It is not only that nations demand room for their homeland which others envy, a sense of territory which we have inherited from our animal forebears, but that nations have long histories and living cultures which are part of their life and cannot be ignored without danger of disintegration. The contemporary British difficulty of finding a national role for itself after giving up the world's largest empire should remind us

---

[1] *Epistle to Diognetus*, 5–6, abridged. Quoted from C. H. Dodd, *Christianity and the Reconciliation of the Nations*, SCM Press (1952), p. 8.

that a facile approach to reconciliation is useless. Ignorance or detached moralizing or idealistic indifference to the fact of power make some Christian comment valueless.

In his lectures *Love, Power and Justice*, Paul Tillich drew attention to the inadequacy of cheap easygoing love in social and political reconciliation:

> A love of any type, and love as a whole if it does not include justice, is chaotic self-surrender, destroying him who loves as well as him who accepts such love. Love is the drive for the reunion of the separated. It presupposes that there is something to be reunited, something relatively independent that stands upon itself. Sometimes the love of complete self-surrender has been praised and called the fulfilment of love. . . . The chaotic self-surrender does not give justice to the other one, because he who surrenders does not give justice to himself. It is justice to oneself to affirm one's own power of being and to accept the claim for justice which is implied in this power. Without this justice there is no reuniting love, because there is nothing to unite.[2]

Because problems of love, power and justice are always involved in the work of reconciliation, the growing together of the nations will always demand risk and effort. Christ's blessing in the Sermon on the Mount, as has already been noticed, was not for the passive but for the peace-*makers*. In spite of all the ambiguities, personal and national, in the careers of Livingstone, Gordon and Lugard, to name three of the creators of the British Empire in Africa, each had a genuine desire to reconcile, to bring peace and good government and to end slavery. They had a sense of responsibility towards Africa and not only to Whitehall, derived from their understanding of the purpose of life itself.

Reconciliation between nations needs not only explorers and soldiers but the detached, humorous and humane administrators who can appreciate the differences between nations. Living in a developing country moving towards independence can be bizarre. 'We work in two worlds, both real,' said one of the last British heads of an African university. 'One day total co-operation and friendliness – the next the most emotional storms.' But this did not prevent his sharing with his African colleagues

[2] P. Tillich, *Love, Power and Justice*, Oxford (1960), pp. 68–9.

all the humour which could be derived from the procession of notables who descend by air on the developing countries, including the UN Secretary General and the Moderator of the General Assembly of the Church of Scotland. How should the latter be treated, formally or informally? 'Let us see whether he gets out of his car or alights – then we will know.' He *alighted*. Behind the dignified courtesy of the British-African reception party was a new hidden bond – the chance to laugh together afterwards at the pomposity of the great.

One contemporary worker for reconciliation in Africa, whose full stature remains to be recognized, was Carey Francis, for many years headmaster of the Alliance High School in Kenya. He believed in the young men of Kenya when very few people were convinced that they were capable of the highest professional achievements. A young Kikuyu boy, agonizingly frightened, bare-footed and homesick, would come to school to be greeted at the railway station by the headmaster, who helped to carry his bags into the van (the first white man he had ever seen carrying luggage) and asked his Christian name, and remembered it. When Kenya became independent Carey Francis never hesitated to criticize old boys who were in the government if they fell beneath his exacting standards, but he lived on in Kenya, respected and admired, and the example of his strong character and the memory of his abrasive attacks on the sinful or the second-rate live on in the minds of hundreds of East African leaders.

I once met Carey Francis at the Alliance High School when Kenya was on the verge of independence. He was in despair. Though he had trained most of the African leaders who were then negotiating with the British, he felt that they were far too bombastic and self-important. He seemed to dread what his former pupils would do and looked back nostalgically to an earlier simpler time when British rule was not questioned. The teacher who had done as much as any single man to prepare the new rulers for their task was afraid of what they would do with their freedom.

But when Kenya became independent and he retired from the Alliance High School, he went to work at Pumwani Secondary

School and died still in harness. Although Kenya was asserting itself in ways he did not appreciate, and its new rulers demanded salaries and cars and comfort Carey Francis never expected for himself, he would not leave the country, and remained a friendly critic and fellow-worker, believing in Kenyans with an obstinate hopefulness. His funeral in 1966 was one of the most moving African-British occasions in the whole history of East Africa. Bitter political opponents were among the old boys who acted as pall bearers, including Mr Njonjo, the Attorney General, Mr Oginga Odinga, the extremist leader of the Opposition, and Mr Tom Mboya, the brilliant Minister for Economic Planning. A cabinet meeting was adjourned and the House of Representatives stood in silence in his memory – a mark of respect normally reserved for its members and for Heads of State. The old headmaster, paternalistic, convinced of the goodness of the British Empire, united the African nationalists because they sensed that beneath what was unacceptable had been an unshakable belief in them as individuals. Here was a man who had faced British officers if he believed that they had been unjust in the emergency and had also faced African crowds if he believed that they had elected 'Liars, drunkards and cheats', as he once described several recently elected politicians to a packed meeting of their supporters.

The funeral speeches and sermons detailed some of the secrets of this reconciling life. The Secretary to the President said that

he was the first European who called me an 'ass' kindly. . . . An essentially simple man, he never understood that large organizations have motivations, dynamics and momentums of their own quite apart from those of individuals. To him the British Empire and the English Public Schools were good institutions because he had faith in the goodness of the individuals who comprised those institutions. It was only when, during the Emergency (Mau Mau), he was appalled by the cruelties and injustices of the British Authorities, that he began to question his faith in the moral purpose of Colonialism. In keeping with his character he saw the national struggle in terms of its effects on individuals. He saw the treatment of individual nationalists by the authorities as evil, and with his characteristic lack of compromise, he protested with all the eloquence of moral indignation against the Authorities.

The Minister of Education spoke of his

efficiency, clearmindedness and devotion to Christian and human values. . . . He came from being a Senior Wrangler to be a mere simple C.M.S. missionary primary teacher at Maseno, a very remote place in Kenya. His humility was indeed outstanding. He was one of the very few headmasters I have come across who are humble enough to apologize to their pupils. This to me is a great gift and a lesson I shall always treasure. . . . Kenya is grateful to men like Carey Francis, who believed in our people and our future at a time when it was not fashionable to do so. He stands out as a shining example of the friendship and co-operation that is possible between men of all nations if goodwill and understanding are there.

Carey Francis had known all his boys' names and in his first week of his first term a new boy discovered that the headmaster was a friend who cared about him as an individual and wanted to know him and to treat him as an equal. To be called an 'ass' as a boy or to be denounced for bombastic language after you had become a cabinet minister, could not break that kind of relationship. There was nothing cold or clinical about Carey Francis. He wanted his Kenyan boys to be fine Christians, he applied the same strict standards to himself, and when he died more than half the Kenya Cabinet had been his pupils. 'Even in his death,' a leading civil servant said, 'he united us'.

The death of Carey Francis marked the end of an era in Kenya, his work and friendship have left behind in the characters of the new rulers the tradition, in the words of Dr Joseph Mungai, at that time in the University at Makerere, that Christians should be people of definite action with qualities which could be harnessed for courageous and manly leadership. Reconciliation between the nations can no longer be based on the paternalistic work of the headmaster, but will require the same open honesty and frank friendship which shone through Carey Francis.

The days are over when British Christians can be heads of universities or schools in Africa, but the churches still have an urgent task to encourage men and women to fill other posts, especially where technical knowledge rather than administrative authority is required. Voluntary Service Overseas does far more than pious resolutions passed by church assemblies to heal divisions, and the young men and women, if they can go out without arrogance, have the best chance because they are not tempted to stand on their dignity.

One African Methodist leader, who spent a year in England on an exchange scholarship provided by the World Council of Churches, was asked what he had learnt: 'that the British have worries and need looking after' was his surprising reply. He had imagined that the administrators and missionaries whom he had known in Kenya were strong men without problems. He learnt that the European Christians who go out to East Africa, and whom he still wanted to welcome, will have to be looked after by the Africans they serve. By understanding the weaknesses of the British he had realized that as they had to be supported, to receive from Africans as well as to give, the relationship between the races could be on the basis of mutual acceptance of each other as they were. He had begun to understand reconciliation at a much deeper level.

The churches still have political influence in many countries, especially in Western Europe and America, countries far wealthier than the developing nations of Asia, Africa and South America. Here reconciling love must be expressed in a struggle for far greater economic justice which will give freedom to the countries where education, housing and medical services are all in short supply. This needs to be seen as a spiritual duty as directly concerned with God's will as those questions which occupy so much of the time of church assemblies today – methods of church government, forms of worship, reunion and inter-communion. Fortunately, the teaching of the Old Testament prophets and of Christ himself brings both Jews and Christians back, again and again, to the righteous law of God which is creatively guiding all men towards the unity in which everyone is fulfilled – the Kingdom of God.

Only occasionally do Christian leaders and Christian congregations realize that love on the grand political scale is justice and that Christians must be concerned in politics to see that those whose political lobby is weak – the aged, the young, the mentally sick, and the under-developed countries among them – receive a fair proportion of attention. Many Christians who agree that their task is to be ministers of reconciliation, still see this in entirely individualistic terms and do not realize that the reconciliation of nations also demands political justice. Before and during the Second World War William Temple was leading British Christians to a new social commitment and perhaps only now is his message being understood.

If we have been right to suggest that reconciliation always involves listening and understanding the real facts we must begin by realizing how the economic development of the world is bearing unfairly upon the under-developed nations, and the inequality is still growing. The facts are staggering. In the USA and Britain there is one doctor to every 1,500 people, whereas in Indonesia there is one doctor for every 71,000 people, and yet we still import doctors from India and Pakistan. In West Europe life expectancy is 65 but in India it is only 35 – reminiscent of the expectation of life among the workers in Sheffield one hundred and fifty years ago, when the Industrial Revolution was uncontrolled in its exploitation of the workers. Literacy in the developed countries is almost universal but in the world as a whole only 40 per cent can read. No wonder much of Asia has ceased to regard America and the West as friends to be copied and looks upon them as rich men to be envied.

Today reconciliation must be seen in secular and economic terms as well as in terms of religious conversion if the Christian Gospel that Christ died for all men is to be sincerely preached as God's word to the nations. Perhaps it is providential that just at the moment when we are beginning to think in terms of secular redemption we have been given the technical skill to increase our aid to the under-developed countries. But we are bound to feel baffled. 'Can I do anything worth while?' Even the most powerful people, the Premiers and the Presidents, appear to be in the grip of events rather than controlling them. This feeling of helplessness is especially strong for the plain man in Great Britain, as the last withdrawals from direct overseas responsibility mark the end of the empire.

Every Christian in fact has three tasks which are not beyond his capacity and which are the putting into hard practice that calling to be the 'soul of the world' which *Epistle to Diognetus* outlined long ago. The first is the duty of self-education, the second the need to serve, the third the maintenance of the vision of international reconciliation.

Self-education means more knowledge and experience of other nations and their different ways of life and more friendship with individuals and groups. If every Christian family and congregation is to become a laboratory of international and ecumenical understanding we must know much more about each other. Fortunately the younger generation will contain far more linguists than ever before and there will be much more chance of real appreciation when nation can actually speak to nation.

Parish meetings and groups which undertake this task must be prepared for open controversy between the races – the meetings will not always be cosy. Editors of Christian newspapers or parish magazines which open their letter columns to the repressed antagonisms which infect both majority and minority groups will be criticized for encouraging the inevitable backlash. But a friendly community is the very place where antagonisms can be expressed and complaints of racial discrimination got off the chest, considered and discussed. Here the evidence can be assessed and answers given and remedies considered. In discussions of race relations there are always some on both sides whose motto seems to be 'My mind is made up: don't confuse me with facts.' To eradicate racial prejudice from either black or white will require a courage and a frankness which we have hardly begun to develop.

But when there is a real desire to be open, the defensive barriers fall and one nation can bring out the best in another nation. The expansive sunny African has something to teach the well-organized Englishman, the gay and emotional Italian can introduce the dour northerner to a new dimension. Indian, African and American-negro homes often have a free natural love of children, which Europeans may well envy. Though the warning of what can go wrong, shown for instance in E. M. Forster's *A Passage to India*, is needed as a caution that the aim must always be genuine reconciliation, the delight in difference between peoples is a divine gift to aid us in this learning about each other. There is joy as well as drudgery in this task.

Service, like the task of self-education, has begun, but needs to go much further. Many parishes already welcome foreign visitors and have international weekends. Voluntary Service Overseas, Oxfam and Christian Aid already evoke that adventurous idealism which used to go into imperial administration, and commercial and other overseas work can do the same. Christian leaders such as William Paton, Bishops Bell of Chichester, Headlam of Gloucester, or Hunter of Sheffield, did 'link work' of real importance.

Can this approach become much more normal instead of being the exception? Why do not more parishes have group holidays abroad and arrange to meet the parishes where they are staying? May not these be the contemporary pilgrimages, which are the real replacements of the old journeys to Jerusalem or Walsingham? Could all ministers in training spend a few months working for a foreign church? Could parishes give a higher priority to their support of churches overseas?

There are great rewards for this. One congregation decided to send its 1967 Easter offering to an ordained lecturer at an African university who had begun to build up a house church congregation in his own home, to which he ministers in his spare time from his university work. They received the following letter of thanks, which reveals the hope of reconciliation which even a small gift can nourish:

I can now gleefully report that the £30 has been credited to my account in Lusaka and I have been able to make over that sum to the Chelston Christian Centre Committee. They are of course most grateful and delighted, as together with the other monies we have been able to raise we now have enough to go ahead and put up a roof on steel legs so that we can begin to break down the ghastly barrier that exists between all sorts of sections of the community; tribal barriers, racial barriers, cultural barriers, income barriers, denominational barriers – the lot! All in microcosm in the small community of about 5,000 to whom I try to minister.

We see the work developing not only evangelistically, though rather to my surprise I find that it is there I put the first emphasis, but also in trying to serve the whole community and the whole personality of each member of it. It is probably difficult for people who have had no first-hand experience of Africa to get on the right wave-length about it. For instance I heard last week that the child of a Permanent Secretary is in hospital with kwashiorkor, a particularly nasty nutritional deficiency disease. If that is the case at that end of the social and income scale, you can imagine what it is like with people earning less than £20 a month who have come in from the bush quite recently and have very little help in adjusting to urban patterns of life on a community level. Visiting in the township is horrifying, discovering that the old tribal and village *koinonia* has broken down so completely so quickly that people no longer know the names and occupations and habits of their next-door neighbours. When you compare the marvellous corporate community spirit of the village with the bleak individualism of the urban townships, it really makes one ask fundamental questions about economic development and the consequent re-organization. So anything the Church can do to overcome these barriers that are being erected round people seems to me to be fundamentally worth doing.

In the meantime we are celebrating the eucharist every Sunday in a funny little school room which requires three-quarters of an hour's application of duster and mop by me before it is fit to use. But so what! Since we started we have doubled the African congregation in a matter of weeks and at last we are managing to replace those ghastly nineteenth century hymn tunes with some Chinsenga and Chinyanja hymns which evoke much more readily not only the environment in which the mass is being said, but also the corporate devotion of the bulk of the congregation.

Self-education and service depend in the end on the vision of the reconciliation, for without it we shall-Jonah-like-cry off involvement, forget the Old Testament teaching about the stranger within the gate and refuse to hear the risen Christ's call to go into all the world. When we choose to see the vision we shall realize that all men are involved in finding and living the good life and will welcome those who will share the joys and insights and questions of that search. The hatreds and complexities of modern international politics require a certain simple determination to reconcile, which is ultimately based on the vision of humanity as one family of God's children.

5

THE CHURCH: RECONCILIATION
THROUGH RESURRECTION

DISUNITY is baffling for Christians, and especially for younger Christians. The Church of all institutions in the world says most about forgiveness and unity but is divided and maintains its divisions with pathetic insistence. Until John XXIII became Pope no bishop of the Eastern Orthodox Church had been officially received in Rome since the late middle ages. Even in England, which prides itself on its tolerance in political and social life, there are still rules about inter-communion based upon deeply-felt theological convictions which prevent many members of the Church of England from receiving communion with other Christians with whom they share so much. Men who in the eyes of contemporaries have been among the most devoted disciples of Christ in the twentieth century – John XXIII, De Chardin, Bonhoeffer, Schweitzer, William Temple, Martin Luther King and Kagawa – could never share the highest Christian worship together. The contrast between the churches' preaching of forgiveness and their own conduct as institutions strikes the younger generation, which is not set in its ways, as difficult and damping, when the need for holiness and unity in bringing the Gospel of Christ to fresh generations should be paramount.

It is true that we have moved towards greater friendship and travelled far in the last hundred years. To give one instance: Christopher Wordsworth, Bishop of Lincoln and founder of Lincoln Theological College, used the word 'anti-Christ' when describing the Roman Catholic Church, and supported one of his clergy who denied the right of the relations of a Free Church minister to inscribe the word 'Reverend' on his tombstone.

Today his college welcomes visiting Roman Catholic lecturers and students and has an ecumenical lecturer, who is a Methodist minister, on its staff, and in this is typical of the gradual movement of reconciliation among the ministers of the Christian churches. In Dr Johnson's words, 'A man must keep his friendship in repair.' At last Christian ministers are beginning to repair their friendships across those denominational walls which were erected at the Reformation and after more recent quarrels.

Laymen today have gone much further. Fortunately, even in the hard days of penal laws, Catholic and Protestant neighbours often remained friends. In the present century Anglicans and Free Churchmen have grown together. A Lincoln business man described this change of attitude from the days when he had been brought up to think that the parish church was about as pernicious as the public house in this way:

We were still influenced by all the misunderstanding and hurt of the eighteenth and nineteenth centuries between Anglican and Free Church people. Perhaps Lincoln, a Cathedral City and especially with its 'up hill' and 'below hill' tradition, was more divided than the average town. . . . But the very fact of our Cathedral, reminding one daily of a one-time glorious unity of purpose in creating and worshipping, always seemed to call me to seek a way through this unseemly and distressing division.

In 1925 I spent some time working on the staff of the Children's Special Service Mission on the Sands, during two summer holidays. This really was a team effort and a tremendous ecumenical experience. The years 1929–39 were spent hard at work in Congregational Church circles. I could never see the point in leaving one section for another of the divided Church. The war experience (R.N. 1940–1945) once again brought serious discontent about our disunion. It was eighteen months in the Kola Inlet in North Russia, and later service in S.E. Asia that brought me in close fellowship with three other young Christians – Church of Scotland, Anglican and R.C. The first two I am still in touch with and have seen them both during the past two years. The R.C. was lost on active service during a convoy home from N. Russia. There was no padre allowed by the Russians on our shore establishment, and three of us worked together, often against rather difficult circumstances, to keep our Company, particularly the younger lads, in healthy form and outlook in every way. There was one memorable occasion when, after a badly mauled convoy came in, we booked the Russian Fleet H.Q. Cinema. A R.N. Chaplain had sailed in with the Squadron and a Communion Service was held. I believe every man who could possibly be spared attended that Service, and I imagine most sections of the Church would be there. . . .When the War was over our Churches appeared to settle down again to the old denominational ways. But in 1954, after the Evanston Conference, Oliver Tomkins called together a small group and we felt prepared to call the Lincoln churches together, and the Council of Churches was formed. Another milestone was passed.

Two comments on this testimony are relevant. Reunion has always owed a debt to laymen who could pioneer, where ecclesiastical leaders were more cautious. Lord Halifax, the inspirer of the Malines Conversations, the lay founders of the YMCA, Ambrose Phillips, the country squire of Grace Dieu in Leicestershire who did so much for Anglican-Roman relations at a difficult time in the nineteenth century, W. J. Birkbeck, the Norfolk squire who worked for Anglican-Russian Orthodox friendship at the beginning of this century, were all keen laymen who had a vision of Christendom and would press on with a simple faith in Christ's will for unity.

'To settle down to the old denominational ways' was more typical of the churches in England than on the continent. In Germany, where many Christians felt that the foundations had been shaken, the end of the war was seized upon as a chance for formerly distinct traditions to work together and this has developed especially in the great Kirchentags and the Evangelical Academies. In France, Protestants at Taizé and Roman Catholics at Istina have established new centres of ecumenical dialogue. In Great Britain, since the war, there have been courageous experiments and careful work in which the churches have cooperated though without any ecumenical breakthrough: the translation of the New English Bible, the building of Coventry Cathedral, the success of Christian Action, the outburst of the 'New Theology' with the astonishing sales of *Honest to God*, show that the Spirit is at work in the churches. There is a new liveliness which perhaps means that the decades of safety-first are almost over and that from this new life will spring a new demand for 'oneness in Christ'. We have been given new companions in the search for truth and the Christian way, and we mean to keep them in the future. The demand for holiness and self-sacrifice is heard in a new context which makes the denominational barriers appear irrelevant as we realize how much is shared by the churches.

We must remember both lay leadership and the new movements of the Spirit when considering whether reconciliation between the churches has a missionary purpose or is primarily a clerical response to the growing secularization of society and the increasing weakness of the churches – the thesis of an Oxford sociologist, Dr Bryan Wilson. Drawing attention to increasing centralization in administration and in the management of funds, buildings and personnel, Dr Wilson concluded:

> The energy which churchmen have put into the ecumenical movement has perhaps been in rough proportion as they have lost hope of the evangelization of the world. . . . Ecumenism may be a policy not only induced by decline, but one encouraging decline.[1]

Dr Wilson is right to link weakness and religious reconciliation but he does not analyse the connexion in sufficient depth. Reconciliation in the sense of deep friendship is impossible for those who say 'I'm all right, Jack', which may be translated into ecclesiastical terms as 'Outside the flourishing church to which I belong there is no salvation'. It is only when Christians and churches recognize their weakness and failures and puzzles that they can come together. Ecumenism is not primarily self-protection or a defence mechanism but a defeat of pride and a triumph of love. Churches as well as individuals can learn from those words of Paul, 'God chose what is without status by family or birth and the despised in the world, even things that are not, to bring to nothing things that are, so that no human being might boast in the presence of God' (I Cor. 1.28, 29).

It is a hard lesson for the established Church of England, which appears so often at the prestige points of modern society – the Coronation, the House of Lords, the fashionable wedding, the high table, and the launching of ships. Christians, and the churches to which they belong, need to be able to say to each other: 'I decided to know nothing among you except Jesus Christ and him crucified. And I was with you in weakness and in much

[1] B. R. Wilson, *Religion in a Secular Society*, C. A. Watts (1966), p. 176.

fear and trembling.' No doubt established churches in Scotland and elsewhere, and churches in the United States which enjoy a kind of 'social establishment', also need to examine themselves.

God uses 'the things that are not': we have to recognize that Christendom, in the sense of society consciously guided by Christian beliefs, with the Church as the respected paternalistic guide, is one of the things that 'is not'. Its place is being taken by a society which is pluralistic and permissive and, in parts of Europe, by a frankly pagan community. But, despite these changes, Christians are divided by half-conscious memories of wounds inflicted or suffered long ago. The Roman Catholic, looking at a cathedral now used by the Church of England, may feel 'They stole that from us', without consciously framing the words. Nineteenth and even twentieth century Protestant England still has vague memories of Armadas and excommunications and the inquisition, which may be buttressed by fear of the competition of Irish labour or dislike of different standards of living. The radical Christian sees a bishop, Anglican or Roman, in his astonishing clothes and half remembers what Samuel Wilberforce said about evolution or what the Roman bishops did to Galileo, and forgets that there are many bishops for whom Trollopian status has meant nothing. The working-class English Roman Catholic priest, with an overcrowded church in a back street, looks at the Anglican Vicar of the town, always to the fore on Remembrance Sunday and often to be seen in an old school tie, and cannot believe that they are fellow ministers. The Free Churchman remembers that his ancestors were excluded from Oxford and Cambridge and that, although Anglicans no longer make the old exclusive claims, talk of 'priesthood' and 'hierarchy' sound threatening. The non-theological factors working against reunion in England are still very powerful, though the society in which they stood for real injustice is dead.

Though half-conscious folk memories can no more be sponged away from the minds of churches than the subconscious can be excised from the human personality, other memories can be placed beside them. Pope John, who received the Archbishop of Canterbury in every way as a church leader, became, thanks to his simple love and Christian humanity, the Pope for all Christians, just as the Abbé Quoist and Teilhard de Chardin have been Roman Christians who have prayed and thought for us all. Reconciliation comes as much by united work for God in the present as by assessing and recognizing the blame for the past.

Here modern technology is coming to the aid of the churches as they present the Gospel of love in the new contemporary world. Television, the paper-back revolution, the serious newspapers, and the open discussion of religious faith in schools, families, universities and theological colleges ensure that new theological ideas can be considered.

When Christians speak from their own considered experience, first hand, and not primarily as officials of religious organizations, they will find more and more agreement. The radical stirrings in all the churches result from the same desire to proclaim and live the Gospel of the love of God and will eventually break through the inherited mental barriers and lead to a new unity of mind.

In the sixteenth century the sense of a fresh understanding of the Christian Gospel gave the Protestant bodies a common approach to the Bible, despite all their divisions in organization. All recognized the need for inspiration from the Bible if Christians were to have a living faith. Unfortunately the church administrators took fright and tried to restrict the circulation of the Scriptures, imprisoning or even burning the translators. Rogers, one of the Protestant martyrs, who was burnt at Smithfield in the presence of his wife, a baby at her breast, and his ten children, had been interrogated by Bishop Gardiner. Gardiner had said: 'No, thou canst prove nothing by Scripture; the Scripture is dead, it must have a lively expositor.' Rogers replied: 'No, the Scripture is alive.'[2]

What is revealed in this dispute is not only a different experience derived from reading the Scriptures but a difference in approach to the task of the Church. The Protestants were united in their belief that a fresh attempt to live and preach the Gospel was necessary and that maintenance work was no longer sufficient. They did not succeed in creating one system of doctrine

[2] A. G. Dickens, *The English Reformation*, Batsford (1964), p. 132.

or one agreed uniform church or form of worship, but they were at one in agreeing that the Bible must have a new place, and this gave Protestantism its cohesion. Today the experience of God as primarily persuasive love, in uniting Christians in many churches, both Catholic and Protestant, does not obliterate their memories of past unreconciled centuries but gives them a hope of life and discipleship together in the centuries to come.

To deal with the quarrels of the past by working together now for the sake of the future will involve us with our immediate neighbours, the people next door. Though it is excellent that Anglicans should be in communion with Anglicans in New Zealand or with Old Catholics in Holland, commonsense suggests that the Roman Catholics, Methodists and Pentecostalists in the same street should be the Christians with whom we should begin if we are concerned with the resurrection of the Church here and now. Here are the immediate opportunities and immediate difficulties. As G. K. Chesterton said, 'I find it easy to love the Eskimos because I have never seen an Eskimo, but I find it hard to love my neighbour who plays the piano over my head too late at night.'

We must recognize the value of the local ecumenical structure, the town and country councils of churches, which have been painfully built up over the years from origins as diverse as a Sands Mission or a joint communion service at the Kola Inlet. The much publicized activity of the papal Secretariat for Unity or the World Council of Churches can leave the laity feeling like God's frozen people.[3] It may be difficult for an Anglican dignitary, with his assured legal position within the establishment, sometimes still dressed in eighteenth century riding kit, to imagine himself sitting under the chairmanship of a Methodist layman with a Baptist secretary to plan what can be done for the Christian mission with far too many parishes and chapels slowly driving both ministers and congregations to resignation and despair. It will be difficult for the dignitary to imagine this if he assumes that only he or an Anglican bishop can take the chair on such occasions. He may simply have to take the lower

[3] See the book with this title by Mark Gibbs and Ralph Morton, Collins, Fontana (1964).

place, keep on attending, being neither chairman or secretary; so centuries of domination of the English religious scene by the establishment will be forgiven. Only by working for the future can memories powerful enough to counteract the memories from the past begin to dominate the Christian communities.

Reconciliation between churches needs to be seen in these personal terms and not primarily as an exercise requiring skilful ecclesiastical carpenters who can reshape the angularities of the existing churches so that they can be made to fit together. This was well put during the Nottingham Faith and Order Conference in 1964 by Father Paul Verghese of the Syrian Orthodox Church of South India. His theme was unity among Christians, a unity that is more than the possession of identical doctrine or church structure and organization. Unity must be sharing in the risen life of Christ in his Church, in his humble, unhypocritical, brotherly love.

This love is not in-turned. To quote Canon T. R. Milford, 'The Church is not like sheep in the sheepfold with their noses together, keeping themselves warm with each other's breath while their tails keep wriggling.' We are to be one in order that the world may believe and that we may serve the world. Our unity must have a quiet forgiving quality, an ethical dimension with a humorous determination to believe the best, which reveals the goodness of Christ.

At one point at Nottingham, Father Verghese quoted the Greek New Testament, and some of his hearers reached for Bibles or better still Greek versions: a learned Roman Catholic priest craned his neck to catch a glimpse of the only Greek text in his view, in the hands of a young Salvation Army lassie. Christendom in that row in the hall relied on the Salvation Army for the scholar's text. For many people Nottingham and other ecumenical occasions begin with a new grasp of the values of other Christians, not with official resolutions but with personal reconciliation based on seeing the truth about each other.

Today unity is growing naturally in a flowering of friendships built on the understanding that we have much to forgive and much to learn. When a Free Churchman in the Dales says 'I'm keenly looking forward to a visit to a Roman Catholic service, a quite new experience for me', generations of mutual misunderstanding and even, in parts of the north of England, years of persecution, are being cut through. The same recovery of a gracious personal relationship was achieved by the young Jesuit who said recently with a smile, 'Splendid man that Midland vicar: he showed me round the parish church and said, "Are you married or single; one has to ask these days?" '

The way to forgiveness begins for churches in the same place that it begins for each one of us.

> But when he came to himself he said. . . . 'I will arise and
> will go to my father, and I will say to him, "Father,
> I have sinned against heaven and before you; I am no
> longer worthy to be called your son" ' (Luke 15.17–19)

Churches, like men, have to face up to the facts about themselves and the way they have treated each other. There was a time when some members of the Church of England looked down on other Christians and talked of 'our incomparable liturgy' or even implied that Anglicanism is a religion designed for 'English gentlemen'. Only when Christians, like our Jesuit friend, can be honest about their weaknesses, only when Christians come to themselves, can they return as sons of their one home and find that their Father is running to meet them.

Nowhere is it more urgent that Christians should face up to the facts about themselves than in the English villages. So often deep social and economic divisions and ancient injustices lie below the ecclesiastical divisions of Church and Chapel. In the Eden valley, and in other parts of Cumberland, bitter disputes over land tenure in the sixteenth and seventeenth centuries contributed to alienation from the Church and a dour support of dissent.[4] Reunion can only come when these facts have been brought into the open and the Church has come to itself, recognizing its involvement in the machinery of government. Perhaps others have to realize that the 'chip-on-the shoulder' mentality is that of the elder brother and not of a son. Then both may be at home together. No casual apologies are adequate; only quiet and costly practical co-operation will help. If Christians

[4] I am indebted here to an unpublished paper on Border Tenant-Right by the Rev. J. Breay.

face the facts and pray for the resurrection of the church, then reunion will come in many northern villages and towns.

Recent research into religious divisions in France has revealed the same deep roots in social injustice. Above the dining-room tables of the Mission de France Seminary at Pontigny, where men are trained to go in groups to the most de-Christianized area of France, there hangs a large multi-coloured map of the pagan areas. One of the explanations of the death of the Catholic Church in these areas is the location of the old royal estates where the unpopularity of the *ancien régime* was greatest. The new Protestant community at Taizé, warned by this and by the fate of the vastly wealthy monastery at Cluny nearby, has taken care not to acquire wide acres but to do its farming through co-operative sharing in the work of neighbouring farmers, not falling into the temptation of adding field to field. It is not sufficient to feel remorse for the sins of one's spiritual ancestors. We have to share a new life together and imprint new memories of co-operation alongside those which are inherited from the past. Handling milk churns in the dairy co-operative can do more to reveal the sharing, caring life of a Christian community than any number of resolutions.

The tendency of so many in the churches to look backwards towards the achievements and quarrels of the past rather than work for the needs of the future still influences even courageous moves towards the healing of divisions. *Towards Reconciliation*, the Interim Statement of the Anglican-Methodist Unity Commission, is an eirenic attempt to deal with controversial questions – the understandings of Scripture and Tradition, Priesthood and Ministry and the Sacrificial Aspects of Holy Communion among others – as well as producing new drafts of the Service of Reconciliation and the Ordinal. The Commission also calls on the two Churches to embark together on new adventures in mission and the service of the community,[5] and 'to serve our nation as one servant church, to teach the people of our nation with one Christian doctrine, and with one voice, to present to the world our one crucified and risen Saviour'.

[5] See pp. 3, 5 and 52 of *Towards Reconciliation*, S.P.C.K. and Epworth (1967).

But the actual treatment of the Christian doctrines of the Bible and tradition, of Ministry and of the Eucharist, are largely in terms of the historic discussions of the past, inevitably so since it is intended to satisfy those in both Churches who fear that some of their inheritance may be compromised. So the Ordination Service is entitled the Ordination of Presbyters, also called Priests, and Presbyter is justified as the most ancient title and as free from those overtones of 'mediatorial intrusion of another man between a Christian and his God' which have led to a dislike of the word 'Priest'. A sympathetic reader will applaud the choice and yet feel that this is an archaic word to use for the Christian minister in modern England. The Unity Commission has inevitably been more concerned with care about the past than with a new forward-looking adventure. To the hope that their report will be accepted by the two Churches must be added the hope that the united church may be able to press rapidly to a new confidence and choose a more contemporary word to describe the ministry.

Of course 'presbyter' has been chosen because for many Methodists and for many Anglicans 'priesthood' is something a minister either has (with 'all believers') or else cannot have at all – for it belongs to Christ alone. For other Anglicans, however, and for some Methodists 'priesthood' is a description a minister would claim as emphasizing the minister's task of standing on the Godward side for man and the manward side for God. Perhaps Bishop Mandell Creighton gave the wisest verdict: 'Priesthood, sacraments, confession are all explicable by themselves. They can be placed in a system which finds room for individual liberty or in a system which excludes it.' Only by working together can the members of the two churches discover that they share the same determination to live together in a church which safeguards liberty and that the ministry exists to serve the church and not to insist that God depends solely on the ministry.

Anglicans and Roman Catholics need to make a special effort to understand Protestant fears of priesthood, and Protestants to appreciate what Catholics value in this function of ministry. The danger was well put in a poster hanging in the porch of Avignon

Cathedral just after the war. 'Mothers give us your sons,' it read; 'when the priest leaves the village, God leaves the village.' Here the slogan suggests that the priest mediates an absentee God who cannot come without him. We know that this is untrue. But the value of the word 'priest' lies in its emphasis on the holiness of God, on his forgiveness and on the sacraments – all that we can see asserted in other gifts of the modern French Church to Christendom. In this emphasis on holiness and forgiveness we can find a joy and a grace which we know instinctively should be gifts of the Spirit. But as our Protestant friends rightly remind us, these are gifts of the Spirit and not privileged prizes presented by specially qualified functionaries.

Our mutual fears, which in England go back past the Reformation to the controversies begun by John Wyclif and continued by obscure but determined critics of the medieval church, will not be resolved overnight. Running joint youth groups, reading the Bible together, joint discussion groups and actually worshipping together are all slowly leading towards union. Those who have experienced united worship in the forces or in the P.O.W. camps or in ecumenical work at home or abroad or in universities and theological colleges, have usually gone furthest in resolving Protestant and Catholic fears. They have discovered in practice what lies behind this emotional word 'priest' and how to avoid the dangers of 'priestcraft' without losing the Godward reference in the ministry.

In the Service of Reconciliation in the reunion suggestions worked out by Anglicans and Methodists no one will be reordained, but the ministries will be reconciled. Anglicans will be given a share in the Methodist ministry and for me personally this will mean the privilege of joining those who have stood outside the Establishment for the sake of the Gospel. Methodists will be given a share in the Anglican ministry which unites them with those churches that treasure continuity with the past through the episcopate.

I believe that it is best that a reunited Church should have a ministry recognized by all from the very beginning, with all the powers and gifts shared amongst all the ministers without distinction; this is the point where the present scheme is bolder than the South Indian scheme. We shall all go to this healing service with the future, not the past, in our minds, not asking what was the status of those kneeling around us but praying that we may be recreated for work together in the reconciled church. God will be freeing us all to walk and work together and it is psychologically inept and theologically faithless to see the service as in some way regularizing or still worse criticizing the past.

A minister of the Church of England may see the Service of Reconciliation like this:

When I was ordained deacon and priest the Bishop laid his hands on me. These hands created a personal relationship which exists to this day. I look upon him as my Father in God. They were also, in my mind, the hands of Jesus Christ ordaining me for service in his Church. When the Presiding Minister of the Methodist Church, at the Service of Reconciliation, lays his hands on me, he will not be a rival Father in God: he will be another Father in God. I hope that there will be a personal relationship like the one which I have now with the Bishop who ordained me. They will be the hands which represent the reconciled Church healed from its bitter divisions, commissioning me afresh for service. They will be the hands of Jesus Christ. . . . Hands conveying a fresh gift of the Spirit for fresh work in the contemporary world.

What will the new church look like? This is the question which needs an imaginative answer. If we could see a compelling picture of the Church of the future, I believe that we would be very much closer to realizing it. But we are inhibited by fears. We are afraid that we shall be absorbed. We are afraid that my Church, my Chapel, my College, my Conference, will be closed. On this question of absorption a West Country Methodist layman, D. F. Nash, said:

When a Cornish housewife puts a pinch of saffron into her cake-mixture she is not 'afraid' it will be absorbed. She knows it will be. And that it will flavour and colour all those delicious cakes and buns that will presently come out of the oven. Was not this John Wesley's idea? And might it not be the Holy Ghost's idea today, for every parish in England?[6]

The story of the Church of South India, as revealed in Bishop Lesslie Newbigin's *A South India Diary*,[7] does show that the different elements of the uniting churches have been combined

[6] D. Foot Nash, *Their Finest Hour*, Epworth (1964), p. 118.
[7] SCM Press (revised ed., 1960).

in a new kind of unity, which has been much more effective than the divided churches. If we think less about our fears we shall see instead a new church which may bridge the gap between organized religion and the masses of the people of this country.

We can prepare for the united church now, though some reforms, such as the Church of England's relation to the State, must wait for reunion. Any disestablishment or re-establishment will require the co-operation of other churches. But we can start at once to reform our worship. Can Anglicans make rather more use of spontaneous prayer within their services? Can Methodists make rather more use of the ancient living liturgies of Christendom? We can reform our organization. It is particularly urgent that all new churches should not be planned without full co-operation. What will our children say to us if we have made the union of future generations more difficult by putting church against chapel across the new roads of the new estates?

Can theological faculties in the universities help the reunion movement even more than they have? Perhaps if the inter-denominational faculties of the British universities could discover whether they could worship together, possibly even at the Eucharist, this would help the less articulate and more conservative parts of the Church. Would it be possible to submit to such a united faculty which worships together questions on reunion in a particular locality, in the same way as a farmer might submit a problem to a university farming research institution? Above all, can the faculties help the Church to have more vision of its future shape?

My own personal vision is built round the Service of Reconciliation. It would happen all over England, sometimes in a Methodist Central Hall, sometimes in a Town Chapel, sometimes in a Village Church. Here long rivalries would die; families and communities long divided by religion would come together. When the great reunion of the Scottish Churches took place in 1929, the two processions met outside St Giles and sang together:

> Behold how good a thing it is
> And how becoming well
> Together such as brethren are
> In Unity to dwell.

(And one fine old Scottish woman had to send for the doctor as the intensity of her joy was so great that her blood pressure became dangerous.) If these services happened all over England, even our restrained country would catch the mood of joy and mutual reconciliation. Here would be a second spring for the English Church, once again strong enough to stand for the things of God – a Church in which we should be released and inspired to go forward together.

In a famous phrase the Lord of the Church said 'I am among you as he that serveth' – 'as the waiter', to quote Dr C. H. Dodd's suggestive translation. The Church is the one historic human institution founded on the conviction that love has been revealed as the meaning and purpose of life and the function of the Church is to 'wait' on the human family to remind it of this fact. And not only to remind but to help humanity to adventure itself in this vision of love and to worship the vision. The Church, like the Lord, is not concerned to make claims for itself but to make claims for life and for what lies beyond life.

The Church today can only preach this supreme Gospel if it will practise it – by being one, by being reconciled. Roman and Protestant, Orthodox and Pentecostalist must come together. No endowments, no legal establishment, no venerable traditions or radical theologies can save it, if it rejects reconciliation – for that is its reason for existence. Has it the faith and courage to allow the victorious Lord of Easter to break the inherited seals and to give it the fresh, joyful and unifying life which flows from the one God of all mankind?

6

REALITY BEFORE RECONCILIATION

THE old insight that there can be no atonement without sacrifice, without painful experience and difficult growth, has often in practice been more effectively expressed by the poets than the preachers. Wilfred Owen's poems, incorporated in Benjamin Britten's *War Requiem*, shatter complacency and arouse active compassion, where more explicitly 'theological' exposition fails.

Novelists who start with life as it is actually being lived in this violent world can make us see the cost of forgiveness. In the recent best-seller, *To Kill a Mocking Bird*,[1] where the theme is racial tension in a sleepy town in the deep south, the reconciling work of the quiet lawyer includes sitting with a gun on his knees outside the prison all night to prevent the accused negro being lynched by the white mob.

The greatest poets, authors and artists have returned again and again to the theme of reconciliation, describing what would be missed by a more superficial attitude, prepared to see life as it really is and not as we would like it to be. Goya's war paintings and Picasso's *Guernica* reveal the consequences of violence, and the naked brutality of the principalities and powers more vividly than any sermon. *Lolita*[2] says more about bondage than many of the commentators who have tried to interpret St Paul's reflection, 'Wretched man that I am! Who will deliver me from this body of death?' (Rom. 7.24).

Shakespeare approached reconciliation in human life from many angles and his plays explore its agonies and hopes and frustrations. He portrays Hamlet caught between the natural

[1] Harper Lee, Heinemann (1960).
[2] V. Nabokov, Weidenfeld & Nicolson (1959).

desire for revenge, implicit in the classical concept of a son's duty to his father, and the humane Christian concept of forgiveness and reconciliation, a dilemma which reveals to him the uncertainties of his own character. There is no reconciliation between Hamlet and his enemies in this life, and at the climax, in the final scene, Hamlet feels he leaves behind him a wounded name.

The quarrels and reconciliations which are kept on a trivial level in the comedies dominate each of the tragedies. King Lear is portrayed as a man who could only be reconciled with Cordelia when he had come to himself and had been shaken out of his complacency and almost out of his sanity.

> I am a very foolish, fond old man,
> Fourscore and upward, not an hour more or less;
> And, to deal plainly,
> I fear I am not in my perfect mind.

But then it was too late and Shakespeare shows the king and his daughter reconciled, but only at the moment of death. Even the old king's hope of life together in prison was not to be satisfied.

> Come, let's away to prison;
> We two will sing like birds i' the cage;
> When thou dost ask me blessing, I'll kneel down
> And ask of thee forgiveness; so we'll live,
> And pray, and sing, and tell old tales, and laugh
> At gilded butterflies. . . .

Shakespeare emphasized that the rack of this tough world is so harsh that the king's longing for reconciliation could not change the consequences of the past, and there were to be no happy days together.

The question whether Hamlet or King Lear (or Macbeth or Othello) are reconciled to themselves is left to each member of the audience to decide and will depend upon the total impression made by the character upon him. Hamlet is still anxious and the final scene is left ambiguous. In some of the last plays (e.g. *The Tempest*) reconciliation comes through the marriage of the children of enemies as though to suggest that problems too bitter for one generation may be resolved by the next. Ferdinand and Miranda, and especially their children, may create a brave new world beyond the possibility of the older generation.

A few years later another poet also turned to the theme of reconciliation. George Herbert was haunted all his life by bouts of depression and fears that he would never become what he had it in him to be. Like John Donne, the greatest of the metaphysical poets, Herbert will always illuminate any exploration of the experience of alienation and failure, around which some of his greatest and simplest poems revolve. As we shall see, he handed them on shortly before his death because he hoped that they might help others to find freedom.

George Herbert's poems entitled *The Temple*, as well as his account of the life of the country parson in *A Priest to the Temple*, go deep into the meaning of forgiveness, reconciliation and acceptance, as Herbert himself experienced them. He was the younger brother of Edward Herbert of Cherbury, one of the most brilliant of the courtiers and diplomatists of the Stuart court and usually named the father of English deism. George Herbert shared his brother's brilliance and ambition and was public orator at Cambridge before he was persuaded by Nicholas Ferrar to consider the Christian life more seriously. He took orders and became, first, prebendary of Lincoln and then vicar of Bemerton in Wiltshire, where he died at the age of forty in 1633, a few years before the outbreak of the civil wars. His writings reveal that below the surface of his uneventful life there was a painful struggle with ambition and the fear of self-frustration. It was hard for him to accept the obscurity and apparent powerlessness of the country parson's life but this problem of ordination was less important than his effort to come to terms with himself. Herbert was sophisticated, musical, well aware of all the cross currents of metaphysical questionings in the court and the universities of his day. His illnesses and his bouts of depression fed his self-distrust which could not be cured by any dogmatic version of Christianity as taught in Rome or Geneva; these he found intellectually unconvincing. He might have lapsed into total self-despair, but instead he came to speak to God with a vivid directness.

> Though my sins against me cried,
>   Thou didst clear me;
> And alone, when they replied,
>   Thou didst hear me.[3]

Herbert was fortunate to have experienced and reflected on so much of contemporary life. Unlike some of the court writers, he was not only supremely intelligent but had an ingrained sense of the English common life and could speak in a popular, homely style, for, as he said himself, 'I like our language.' Perhaps he owed some of his directness to the tradition of the popular medieval preacher, some to the strong terse English of the Bible and the Book of Common Prayer and some to the life of the country parson who must live and speak openly, as he is, without pretence.

In his poems he tried to work out his conflicts with himself, and his doubts about the God who hides himself, and the difficulties of following the way of serenity and love and lack of self-concern. He tried to resolve the conflicts and find a way of reconciliation, but because of his realism this is no cheap reconciliation. No doubt the reason why Charles I in prison and so many others during the civil wars found these poems so liberating was that here was a man proving his faith by his own experience and at first hand. As Bonhoeffer's *Letters and Papers from Prison* speak to the twentieth century, so and for the same reason George Herbert's poems spoke to the seventeenth.

When he sent his poems to Nicholas Ferrar a few weeks before his death this message accompanied the manuscript:

> Sir, I pray deliver this little book to my dear brother Ferrar, and tell him he shall find in it a picture of the many spiritual conflicts that have passed betwixt God and my soul, before I could subject mine to the will of Jesus my Master; in whose service I have now found perfect freedom; desire him to read it: and then, if he can think it may turn to the advantage of any dejected poor soul, let it be made public; if not let him burn it; for I and it are less than the least of God's mercies.

In several of his poems Herbert described his feelings of alienation and frustration; he feels unreconciled to himself and

3 Praise.

to God. *Affliction* (*I*) ends with an astonishing verse about alienation turning to acceptance.

> Yet, though thou troublest me, I must be meek
> > In weakness must be stout.
> Well, I will change the service, and go seek
> > Some other master out.
> Ah my deare God! though I am clean forgot
> > Let me not love thee, if I love thee not.

One of the most moving accounts of the blankness of prayer which does not seem to work and the freemasonry of discouraged Christians who find prayers so difficult, especially prayer 'unearthed' in ordinary life, is the chapter entitled 'Worldly Holiness' in John Robinson's *Honest to God*.[4] Most Christians should be willing to admit openly and calmly that this is or has been their experience. George Herbert made his own confession of the difficulty of prayer in his poem, *Denial*, where his broken versing underlines his experience of the broken relationship to God which is linked to a broken relationship with himself; for Herbert rightly saw that prayer is both talking to God and talking to oneself, it is both listening and asking.

> When my devotions could not pierce
> > Thy silent ears;
> Then was my heart broken, as was my verse;
> > My breast was full of fears
> > And disorder.
>
> My bent thoughts, like a brittle bow,
> > Did fly asunder:
> Each took his way; some would to pleasure go,
> > Some to the wars and thunder
> > Of alarms.
>
> As good go any where they say,
> > As to benumb
> Both knees and heart, in crying night and day,
> > COME, COME, MY GOD, O COME!
> > But no hearing.
>
> O thou that shouldst give dust a tongue
> > To cry to thee,
> And then not hear it crying! all day long
> > My heart was in my knee,
> > But no hearing.

4 SCM Press (1963).

> Therefore my soul lay out of sight,
> > Untuned, unstrung:
> My feeble spirit, unable to look right,
> > Like a nipt blossom, hung
> > > Discontented.
>
> O cheer and tune my heartless breast,
> > Defer no time;
> That so thy favours granting my request,
> > They and my mind may chime,
> > > And mend my rhyme.

Herbert's poems are intelligent, witty, sometimes brilliant in their skilful construction, and the best are direct – spoken sometimes to the reader, sometimes to Herbert himself, sometimes to God. They are only rarely metaphysical in the sense of being artificial, and his most successful poems seem to be wrung out of the poet himself, as though they arose from a realm in his personality over which he had only partial control and to which he listened intently. He believed in self-examination of his own motives so that he could grow in self-knowledge. In one of his longer poems, full of avuncular advice such as 'Drink not the third glass' and 'Play not for gain, but sport', he included this verse:

> By all means use some times to be alone.
> Salute thyself: see what thy soul doth wear.
> Dare to look in thy chest; for 'tis thine own:
> And tumble up and down what thou findest there.
> Who cannot rest till he good fellows find,
> He breaks up house, turns out of doors his mind.

In his own experience Herbert had found that reconciliation needs quiet, reflection and meditation for which even the happiness of friendship cannot be a substitute, and may even be an escape mechanism. Herbert urged his readers to dare to know themselves, though this meant facing the despairs and hatreds and sheer blocks of boredom which we may find there. It is at this level that the Spirit of God must work if reconciliation is to come, and the Christian become a reconciled person like his Lord.

Herbert saw this as the natural place for God's work of reconciliation, since God is the father of Jesus Christ who was found where he was least expected. In his tiny poetic parable entitled *Redemption*, Herbert vividly told the story with all the emphasis on the Lord's anonymous hidden work.

> Having been tenant long to a rich Lord,
>   Not thriving, I resolved to be bold,
>   And make a suit unto him, to afford
> A new small-rented lease, and cancel the old.
>
> In Heaven at his manor I him sought:
>   They told me there, that he was lately gone
>   About some land, which he had dearly bought
> Long since on earth, to take possession.
>
> I straight return'd, and knowing his great birth,
>   Sought him accordingly in great resorts;
>   In cities, theatres, gardens, parks and courts:
> At length I heard a ragged noise and mirth
>   Of thieves and murderers: there I him espied,
>   Who straight, *Your suit is granted*, said, and died.

Herbert's vivid realism about Christ's reconciling work was due to the same experience which underlay the realism of Christ's parables – that he had seen God actually at work. He was rarely concocting skilful analogies or imposing fanciful patterns, and was at his best when observing God at work in the secular material world in which he could be personally known and in which men could, if they would, accept him, each other and themselves.

When Herbert looked at his own life he was deeply dissatisfied because it did not measure up to what he knew the times needed or to the intricate activity of God in giving life to the harmonious and orderly universe.

> All things are busy; only I
> Neither bring honey with the bees,
> Nor flowers to make that, nor the husbandry
>   To water these.

Enemies had wrecked God's intentions, the foundations had been shaken and man lived an alienated and ambiguous life.

> Love built a stately house; where FORTUNE came
> And spinning fancies she was heard to say,
> That her fine cobwebs did support the frame
> Whereas they were supported by the same:
> But WISDOM quickly swept them all away.

Then SIN combined with DEATH in a firm band,
To raze the building to the very floor:
Which they effected, none could them withstand.
But LOVE and GRACE took Glory by the hand,
And built a braver Palace than before.

In his poem on *Providence* Herbert writes that

Only to Man thou hast made known thy ways,
And made him Secretary of thy praise.

Beasts fain would sing; birds ditty to their notes;
Trees would be tuning on their native lute
To thy renown: but all their hands and throats
Are brought to Man, while they are lame and mute.

Man is the world's high Priest; he doth present
The sacrifice for all. . . .

The highest human task is to interpret the harmony which is the divine intention and to act as secretary in passing on God's message and returning the thanks of a grateful creation . . . but the secretary fails. Herbert lived just before the civil war and knew the bitter strains which were beginning to appear in society. He knew, too, from his own experience, how often his own personality was torn by contradictory desires. No doubt when he defined the pastor as 'the deputy of Christ for the reduction of man to the obedience of God' he was thinking of this supreme task of the Christian to be his best self, the self he is meant to be, and to help others to be true to themselves within the divine scheme.

Man's failure was met by Christ in his passion and resurrection. Herbert, like all Christians, felt that his self-distrust was overcome by God coming forward in Christ to his rescue. This was not something done long ago and then, as it were, switched off; long before Calvary God's redeeming love had been felt by the Israelites and now, long after Calvary, the work goes on to make man capable of living within a reconciled universe.

Thy life on earth was grief, and thou art still
Constant unto it, making it to be
A point of honour, now to grieve in me,
And in thy members suffer ill.

And they who lament one crosse,
Thou dying daily, praise thee to thy losse.

In another poem, the *Agony*, Herbert gave a restrained hint that it is in the sacrament of Holy Communion that the reconciling spirit can begin to warm our own characters.

> Who knows not Love, let him assay,
> And taste that juice which on the crosse a pike
> Did set abroach; then let him say
> If ever he did taste the like.
> Love is the liquor sweet and most divine
> Which my God feels as blood, but I as wine.

This sense of the divine acceptance did not come easily or maintain itself steadily even for a character as wise and saintly as George Herbert. He had to discipline his fastidious taste, to learn to listen and attend, so that he could

> enter into the poorest cottage, though he even creep into it, and though it smell never so lothsomely. For both God is there, and those for whom God died.

He said that his poems were a picture of many spiritual conflicts between God and his soul which took place before he could subject his will to Jesus his master, in whose service he found perfect freedom. The reconciler is always on probation.

For Herbert, and for Christians before and since, the divine acceptance is mediated through the Liturgy. His poem *The Sacrifice*, with its repeated refrain, 'Was ever grief like mine?' reflects Herbert's sensitive understanding of suffering for others. He went deep into the images and metaphors, which poets and artists have used to describe the atoning, reconciling work of Christ, in which we see the costliness of God's acceptance of man. *The Sacrifice* is a poem about participation, God's participation in the sufferings of the world and man's need to share with God in this participation. The whole poem draws on the immensely rich imagery of the liturgical keeping of Holy Week, which was alive in the England of Herbert's time and is still available in all Christian communities which give time and imagination to the liturgy today.[5]

Imagination rather than erudition is needed to appreciate the pathos of this poem. The Old Testament references need not

[5] See for a detailed analysis Rosemond Tuve, *A Reading of George Herbert*, Faber (1952).

so much a concordance or a commentary as the willingness to feel life as interpreted in the Christian images of reconciliation with a loving God whom we can know.

Herbert saw the irony of Christ, wholly at the mercy of those he was to liberate, who only knew freedom because God himself has willed them deliverance from bondage so that they could freely respond. It is God who puts himself in man's power though man has no power to be a free person without God liberating him.

> The Princes of my people make a head
> Against their Maker: they do wish me dead,
> Who cannot wish, except I give them bread:
> > Was ever grief like mine?
>
> Without me each one, who doth now me brave,
> Had to this day been an Egyptian slave.
> They use this power against me, which I gave:
> > Was ever grief like mine?

Only when we have had some experience of the imprisoning power of loneliness or the dread of loss and disaster can we appreciate the full force of *An Egyptian slave*. A Yorkshire miner's wife, waiting for her husband to come home from the pit after a reported accident in the deep working, said: 'After this I know what coming out of Egypt means.' And perhaps the power of the image of being rescued from the dark slavery of Egypt helped to reveal the wonder of those moments in life when we are aware of deliverance and reconciliation.

> O all ye who pass by, behold and see:
> Man stole the fruit, but I must climb the tree;
> The tree of life to all, but only me:
> > Was ever grief like mine?
>
> Betwixt two thieves I spend my utmost breath,
> As he that for some robbery suffereth.
> Alas! what have I stolen from you? death:
> > Was ever grief like mine?
>
> They gave me vinegar mingled with gall,
> But more with malice: yet, when they did call,
> With Manna, angels' food, I fed them all:
> > Was ever grief like mine?

Herbert saw Christ as the pioneer who would climb the tree which was life and love for the world but death to him, as the rescuer who would give eternal life in place of death and as the bread of life who would feed man with what he most needed, peace and love. Man chose the violence of crucifixion, the condemnation of Christ with the thieves, and the gift of vinegar mingled with gall, as contrasted with the manna.

The passion stories of the gospels and all the meditations which have grown from them, including Herbert's, which is a re-feeling and restatement of the traditional Holy Week liturgy, point to the same mystery: the costliness of forgiveness, reconciliation and atonement. What ought to be easy, obvious, straightforward, is bought out of suffering, deep sympathy, the willingness to sacrifice. It has to be bought in this way because we know God's love and yet are again and again gripped by our own self-concern and self-interest.

Herbert was aware that Christ's own actions could be interpreted as self-concern, a paranoid self-assertion of being equal with God, who alone can forgive and reconcile.

> Then they accuse me of great blasphemie
> That I did thrust into the Deitie
> Who never thought that any robberie.

Herbert was recalling one of the great Christian themes that Christ, the Son of God, by his very incarnation as well as by the fact that he was on the side of the down-trodden, the friend of publicans and sinners, had not snatched at equality with God. Christ, the reconciler, had not grabbed deity, but being both God and man brings God where he is most needed, to the very centre of fear, sin and death.

> All my disciples fly; fear puts a bar
> Betwixt my friends and me. They leave the star
> That brought the wise men of the East from far.

> Then with a scarlet robe they me array
> Which shews my blood to be the only way,
> And cordial left to repair man's decay:

Ultimate reconciliation always demands courage and the willingness to give nothing less than life itself. There are many first steps to reconciliation, gentleness, courtesy, sensitivity, but when the gulf is great only atonement at risk of life itself can be effective. 'Blood the only way' is the theme of the Gospel, the theme of Herbert's poems, the theme of every deep modern analysis of reconciliation.

Reconciliation, George Herbert knew, requires a passionate caring, an angry determination to smash the barriers, and an ambition to achieve. But finally the work would be done by love, a creative, determined, responsible love.

> Then let wrath remove;
> Love will do the deed:
> For with love
> Stony hearts will bleed.
>
> Love is swift of foot;
> Love's a man of war,
> And can shoot
> And can hit from far.

7

THE SACRAMENT OF RECONCILIATION

In the tiny village of Campitello in the Italian Dolomites, a lorry driver at a building site, whilst backing his vehicle, drove it off the hard ground on to the surrounding muddy slush. The wheels skidded, and as he tried to regain the road the entire village collected, like the chorus entering from the wings at the climax of an opera. There was excited shouted advice, sacks and planks were laid, and several men pushed the ends of posts under the wheels to lever them forward. Then the driver got back into his cab, revved the engine, and leaned out holding up his hand. Everyone paused; he made the sign of the Cross, put his engine into gear and drove off, to the laughter and cheers of the village.

The sign of the cross, before it degenerated into a version of 'thumbs up', was a profound symbol exchanged between the members of a persecuted brotherhood reminding them of their faith in Christ – and for many Christians, including perhaps at times that Italian lorry driver, the sign is still that kind of a symbol. But symbols can degenerate and lose their power; for some Christians this has happened even to the eucharist, which was intended to re-present the whole reconciling work of Christ, his death and resurrection. A deeper appreciation of the task of reconciliation within the life of the Church will certainly involve a renewed understanding of the eucharist as the sacrament of reconciliation.

No one should think that the eucharist is an optional extra if we are to devote ourselves freshly to reconciliation. Paul Tillich, after speaking of the 'death of the sacraments' especially in the Protestant churches, asserted that a disappearance of the sacramental element would lead to the disappearance of Christian worship and finally to the dissolution of the visible church itself.

The African sociologist, Dr K. A. Busia, in his *Urban Churches in Britain*,[1] concluded his sympathetic survey with the verdict that 'they lack the boldness that is born of conviction and faith'. This acute Ghanaian had noticed the criticism from within the churches of their forms of worship; can it be that failure to grasp the resources available through the eucharist has gravely weakened the churches in this country? If Christians are not aware of what they are doing in public worship the divine pressure towards reconciliation may be blocked.

Worship leads to reconciliation because it asserts that there is someone worth acknowledging, who gives meaning to life, who can be glimpsed but not grasped, who is present and yet beyond our understanding. Christian worship, and especially the eucharist, warns us that God is not ourselves on a large scale, is not the 'Daddy' everybody wants, but is holy and righteous and creative beyond our dreams. When we make our own the song of the Cherubim and Seraphim, 'Holy, Holy, Holy', we are asserting that God is wonderfully beyond us. He does not belong to the English or the Western democracies or the communists or the Afro-Asians. He is not destroyed by new theologies proclaiming his death, nor dependent upon old ones with an over-systematic account of his being. No doubt Christians have often spoken as if they carried with them the truth about God, but at the heart of the eucharist they have always known that God was wonderful beyond words, that he cared for all, whether they acknowledged him or not, that he willed the union of mankind and that peace among men was part of his glory.

Worship, and especially the eucharist, leads to reconciliation, not only because it turns us to the God who is beyond us all but because eucharist is the work of the community. The congregation is not a series of isolated individuals, or even groups of families, but it is the People of God, descended from the People of the Old Testament, like them given a 'corporate personality' and like them the object of God's love. As the old Israel felt bound to thank God for its creation as well as its deliverance from Egypt so the Church, especially in its common worship in the eucharist, has felt naturally bound to thank God for bringing

[1] Lutterworth (1966).

85

it out of darkness into his marvellous light and giving his Son to die and rise again. The Church is reconciled to itself, redeemed from its mediocrity, able to face its creaking machinery and endure its timidity because Sunday after Sunday it feels the divine life making it into one body and can offer itself to be a reasonable, holy and lively sacrifice. The life comes through word as well as sacrament in the eucharist, through the sermon as well as through the bread and wine and knits the worshippers into one body, which should be of one heart and one mind.

Unfortunately, teaching and practice have occasionally obscured this principle – that the worship of God leads to reconciliation. A colleague in an east-end Sheffield boys' club, who had a genius for friendship with almost unclubbable boys and had been brought up in a Christian home and had worshipped at his parish church, remarked at a club discussion that even if he joined the 'God-botherers', as he described Christians, he could not take part in the pre-scientific magic of the sacrament. No one had ever taken the trouble to discuss with him the difference between magic, where it is imagined that certain words and actions can compel certain consequences, and sacraments, which are prayers in action, where the Christian people in obedience to Jesus Christ worship God and are knit to him and to each other. No one had interpreted sacraments as declared dependence, effecting and deepening our relationship to God and to each other. He had so much experience of how friendship could be communicated through activities or through gifts – the week at camp in Derbyshire or the book of modern poetry for a sensitive imaginative boy – that it was tragic that he condemned the bread and wine because they were things and could not see them as means of reconciliation in the hands of God.

Perhaps if my friend had been brought up in the Church today he might have found understanding the sacrament to be easier. The eucharist is more often central to the life of the Church, and not an antique rite from an earlier age, as dead as a fly caught in amber, as he had felt it to be. If we could realize that reconciliation is a dominant note of the worship of the eucharist, as dominant as presence, or sacrifice or fellowship, this would make the purpose of this act of worship clearer still. Rather than point to the fellowship of the Church we should point to Christ himself and suggest that the serious love of the unseen Christ is the highest of all reconciling loves –

> Look Father, look on his anointed face;
> And only look on us as found in him.

Joyful and imaginative worship at the eucharist is recreating reconciling communities in many parts of Christendom and perhaps these are as significant as fresh springs as many of the better publicized reforms in the Church. Here is a brief description of one.

Tizard Hall, one of the residential halls in the Imperial College of Science in South Kensington, has no chapel or chaplain, but Holy Communion is celebrated every Thursday morning in term time. Six or seven stories up, looking out over the cranes which are building new halls of residence for the coming generations of science students, a small group of twenty Anglicans and Free Churchmen gather at 8.30 a.m. in one of the open common rooms, whose only decoration happens to be a brass-rubbing of a crusader. We sit in a circle talking, reading the newspaper, gradually getting quieter until far below on the road we can hear a motor bike turning out of Exhibition Road and stopping opposite the lift entrance below. The priest from the University Chaplaincy has arrived.

The service is short and direct. On a plain table there is simply the paten and chalice and the priest wears a stole over his black cassock. It lasts only thirty minutes, yet there is time for the service with a five minute sermon, as well as for silence and a moment for us to greet each other by passing on the kiss of peace by grasping each other's hands. Of course everyone knows each other's Christian name. We stand to receive communion, which is usually administered by a layman, often the Warden of the Hall. After the blessing we have breakfast together, and then men rush off to lectures and labs in many parts of London.

This Holy Communion is holy, though it is not in a church and there is almost no ceremonial or ritual. Here men care about what God is doing, dare to pray to him, and do not feel inhibited by the disbelief and scepticism of so many of their contemporaries. It is concentrated and peaceful even though it is all so direct and uses only half the words of a 1662 service. Its style is modern. You feel that God is available for a technological world and that Christianity can provide a criterion of sensitivity for scientists working on computers as it has for human life in the past.

This was evidently a sacrament of reconciliation. At breakfast afterwards we could immediately talk to each other – though breakfast in university halls is not usually a very sociable meal. It was not only a discussion of the expedition to Iceland or the drive across the Sahara which were being planned for the summer vac. – there was a friendliness in that group which had been built up through those weekly sacraments, surmounting the barriers of different faculties and backgrounds. The fact that this was intercommunion and that some seemed more drawn to an Eastern Orthodox approach to prayer and others were Free Church, made the reconciliation effected in the sacrament the more impressive.

We talked at breakfast about the strain of living in a college with Jews and Arabs in the week of the Jewish-Arab war, about the tensions produced by the very demanding examination system, about the difficulties of deciding about careers when the need for physicists and technologists is so great. Finally the Warden got up and thanked the group and the Chaplain for providing a moment of assured understanding in the college. In all this, it seemed to me as a visitor, divine grace was at work.

In the other six halls of Imperial College, Holy Communion is celebrated once a week and in lecture rooms and laboratories during lunch hours for non-resident students. It is not the only activity of the church in the college. There are 'get-to-know-you' meals at which the chaplaincy priest meets six or seven church members over supper in the refectory and coffee in a student's room; these meetings usually end with Holy Communion and there are, of course, the inevitable late-night discussions and debates.

In a community where so many are engineers, the effective use of materials matters. The use of bread and wine, the material elements, make the eucharist especially significant. It is an assertion that God is involved in the process, concerned with things as well as ideas, as the scientists are concerned with things as well as ideas. Water, bread and wine are not arbitrarily selected for use in the eucharist, they have a natural appropriateness for the worship of the creator and make it clear that our immense human programme for reshaping the world must be seen as a reshaping of God's world for the sake of all his children. The consecration of bread and wine is their setting aside for a new and holy use. This reverent treatment of a tiny but representative part of creation marks what should be the human approach to the whole task of recreating the world, which man at last has the means to do. The dangers of war and dehumanization are there to warn us that we are stewards and that new scientific discoveries can raise really important ethical questions. Man can behave thoughtlessly and ruthlessly towards the creation, as Rachel Carson in *The Silent Spring*[2] and so many others have rightly insisted. The eucharist, by using bread and wine and water, will not allow us to forget that man must be reconciled with God's created world.

The service I have described had no music, but where young groups of Christians in many parts of the world are using new types of music a special effort of understanding among older Christians is needed. It is relatively easy to grasp the purpose of Benjamin Britten's *War Requiem* or to appreciate the power of *The Burning Fiery Furnace* but the efforts made, especially in Germany, to combine the tradition of the Chorale with the complex new serial music require much more knowledgeable sympathy. What is at stake here, and even in the 'pop' services so popular in England, is not the use of new types of music as gimmicks to attract people to the service but that music, especially the most recent music which is most characteristic of our age, should be offered in worship. Music can be prophecy and can communicate in a way in which words sometimes fail. The musicians, including those who are most modern, need to be welcomed and assured that their latest music can be offered in worship, especially at the eucharist. So often since the Renaissance the Church and the artist have drifted apart but faith in the living creative God demands faith in their reconciliation.

[2] Hamish Hamilton (1963).

To understand why the eucharist reconciles means that we should remind ourselves again and again that here is an action which is done rather than a set of words said. F. D. Maurice, perhaps the most influential Anglican theologian of the last century, preaching on the Prayer Book and the Lord's Prayer, drew attention to this fact that we have mentioned already – that the eucharist is prayer in action and not an intellectual formula:

> By Holy Communion (he said) if we use it simply and faithfully, we may overcome that fearful tendency to reduce the laws of the divine Love under the notions and conceptions of our own minds, and that as fatal tendency to separate Christ from the Father, Christ's life from our life, and the life of each member of his body from the life of the rest. . . . Whenever we have begun to notionalize about it, and to disconnect it with the belief of the absolute Love of God, the perfect Sacrifice of Christ, the privilege we possess of presenting our own bodies as sacrifices to Him, its character has perished. . . . We have proof enough in its history that no charm lies in it – considered by itself, apart from God – to preserve us from the most fatal confusion, the deepest moral death; but equal proof that when it is taken as God's method of communicating with His creatures, of unfolding the relation in which he stands to them – when He is believed really to be present in it, and they come really trusting in Him and yielding themselves to Him – it is the most wonderful means of translating words into life, and of reconciling truths which when they are offered as propositions to the intellect, must be contradictory.[3]

No doubt one reason for the curious fact that the eucharist has been found to be so reconciling, but that the divisions over eucharistic theology have been so disastrous, is that the theologians have tried to be too precise and failed to take seriously the impossibility of describing exactly what God is doing in the sacraments. The heart of Christian worship must retain a mystery and we must allow it to speak for itself – or rather to allow God to speak through it. But it is central to the whole work of reconciliation. To quote F. D. Maurice again:

> Ask yourself then solemnly and seriously – 'Can I find Christianity . . . a Christianity of acts, not words, a Christianity of power and life, a divine, human Catholic Christianity for men of all countries and

[3] Quoted by A. R. Vidler, *F. D. Maurice and Company*, SCM Press (1966), p. 126.

all periods, all tastes and endowments, all temperaments and necessities, so exhibited as I find it in this Sacrament?'[4]

Christians in many branches of the Church are experiencing afresh the astonishing creative power of God in the eucharist. It begins with a desire to love and serve God and his people more and it dies whenever people say 'I love my principles more than I love people' – for the highest principle is love and reconciliation. At St Martin-in-the-Fields, Dick Sheppard was instituted fifty years ago with eleven people in an almost empty church, and realized just how much a caring community was needed in the centre of London. When Sheppard had had his vision of tired bits of humanity dropping in there, gradually St Martin's became a place where the eucharist meant home and love. The same transformation has taken place at St Severin in Paris, in a district where hope dies easily. When the church is trying to carry some of the burdens of modern life – loneliness, impersonality, drugs, rootlessness – nothing but a close-knit community is strong enough. On the walls of a small house-church attached to St Severin, below the figure of the Risen Christ, is this inscription: 'Si tu tombes, ne perds pas courage; demeure dans la joie, car Dieu est fidèle.'

Liturgy is coming to life in many communities. On the Sunday I write this, Lincoln theological college has celebrated the eucharist together, with the whole community including the wives and children. Some of the children who are under five are in a crèche nearby, but most are at the service, and the noise they make reminds us that we are one community with the next generation as well as with the surprising selection of the saints of the past our fathers chose for the stained glass window over the altar, who include Melchizedek, Athanasius, Augustine, Thorlak and Bishop Christopher Wordsworth.

This morning, in addition to those training for the Anglican ministry, we welcomed at the service four men training for the Methodist ministry and a Jesuit in training for his ministry. As Lincoln has a Methodist minister as Ecumenical Lecturer, we naturally have many visitors from other churches. The

[4] F. D. Maurice, *The Prayer Book and the Lord's Prayer*, Macmillan (1893) pp. 262 ff.

eucharist remains the centre of our unity, where the prayer of Christ that his followers might be one is most clearly heard and the unhappiness of our divisions most fully felt.

After the eucharist we all have breakfast together, between eighty and a hundred men, women and children – a high point in the week for the children who are scattered at different schools in the city, and perhaps for their mothers who for once have a meal provided for them. Afterwards the men have the chance to worship in different churches in the city – the cathedral, the parish churches, St Hugh's Roman Catholic church, the Free churches, the Quakers and the Pentecostalists, as they themselves decide. This leads sometimes to return visits, so that slowly but surely the unity Christ wishes for his own Body is being achieved.

One of the great difficulties for all parishes and communities where Christians of other churches come to the eucharist, is that the Church of England has not during the last hundred years accepted the practice of intercommunion. This causes misunderstanding and controversy, inside the Church of England itself and especially with the Church of Scotland and the English Free churches, though those Anglicans who oppose intercommunion do not do so because they think non-episcopal eucharists are unreal, but because they believe that Holy Communion should be the sign that full reconciliation in corporate unity has been achieved and should not precede it. Perhaps, however, this view is being overtaken by events, as more and more Anglicans feel it their duty to communicate when invited to the eucharist of a community or conference whose life they have been sharing. It seems, too, as if more non-Anglicans wish to communicate with us than was customary twenty years ago. Perhaps these changes are due not to lax views of the sacrament but to the belief that in the eucharist God is at work as reconciler and that only here, where the saving work of his Son is fully represented, shall we be forgiven our corporate disunity in the past and made into One Body to serve and worship him together in the future.

In one of the earliest prayers about the eucharist found in the *Teaching of the Twelve Apostles*, thanks are given for the eucharist as the means of our reconciliation in these words:

We give thanks to thee, our Father, for the life and knowledge which thou madest known to us through thy servant Jesus . . . . As this broken bread was scattered upon the hills, and was gathered together and made one, so let thy Church be gathered together into thy kingdom from the ends of the earth. . . .

This ancient prayer is being answered as Sunday by Sunday the eucharist recreates a new human community who are friends of God and who find here a new life and a new forgiveness generously given over and over again. It began when God was in Christ reconciling man and creating his Church, and again and again this reconciling love is fanned into flame at this service.

There are many instances of this gracious love, but one quoted by John Wesley in his *Journal* for September 3rd 1739 is particularly vivid and sums up the experience of Christians:

I talked largely with my mother, who told me that, till a short time since, she had scarce heard such a thing mentioned as the having forgiveness of sins now or God's spirit bearing witness with her spirit; much less did she imagine that this was the common privilege of all true believers. 'Therefore,' said she, 'I never darst ask it for myself. But two or three weeks ago, while my son Hall was pronouncing those words, in delivering the cup to me, "The blood of our Lord Jesus Christ which was given for thee", the words struck through my heart, and I knew God, for Christ's sake, had forgiven *me* all *my* sins.'

In these words time seems to stand still . . . perhaps because we know that this is a possibility for each of us and for the Church today.

8

EPILOGUE: THE RISK OF RESURRECTION

WHEN the Christian faith is being argued about and assessed with a new openness and the justification of religion on grounds of habit or convention is felt to be weak, there is always a danger that God may become a problem. When Christians feel the questionings and scepticism of their contemporaries with special acuteness, then to commit oneself to the Christian life may seem to endanger one's integrity or to 'label' oneself as having a closed and unsympathetic mind.

But if reconciliation is at the heart of the Gospel and at the same time central to human existence, to commit oneself to the experiment of reconciliation does not involve a dishonest and improper cocksureness. This is not to accept a newly-made party line, but to work away at the many points where reconciliation is relevant and to accept the responsibilities and even the routine of the community which is committed to reconciliation.

Every Easter this community faces the risk of resurrection, in eucharist and gospel reading, in word and prayer, in drama and in music; there appears a living, surprising, demanding person – Jesus Christ, who has died and risen again and now – like no one else in the world – comes to reveal the way to God and the way to live as a son of God.

No one can give a full acount of how the risen Christ challenges us today. In the story in the gospels he rose unseen and unheard during the night, when human vitality was at its lowest. After the first Easter, men and women became convinced of his presence, not because the felt they could assess him or because they could describe the technique of his resurrection (of that they simply said 'God raised him'), but because as they met him they discovered in themselves, in others and especially in his Church, a new way of living and hoping and believing which they wished to share.

This way of reconciliation at many levels, with God, with oneself, with others, becomes more, not less important, as men discover new sciences and new techniques undreamt of in the New Testament world. The vocation to be a reconciled and reconciling man, seen perfectly in Christ, is still the supreme human vocation for which men need all the resources available – including the resources of the Gospel. The scientifically remade world to which men are increasingly devoted needs the vision, the insights, the control – in a word, the truth of the Gospel, as much as did the earlier and less sophisticated centuries.

Every successive Easter, and every Sunday which is a weekly repeating of Easter, there is the same proclamation of the victory of forgiveness and goodness – and the same promise that the fruits of this victory are available to be shared by those who will walk this same path. It is a joyful proclamation urging us in the first place to live in this way rather than to speculate or to argue. When Christians – and the Church – take this path, then others can understand why the world needs the Gospel. Even small groups living for reconciliation and praying for reconciliation can be effective as words cannot. God knows how many would see the need for reconciliation and would follow Christ's way if his explicit disciples would have the courage of their convictions.

The joy of the eventual victory has never been better described than in some words which link together discipleship, the new world and reconciliation:

> When anyone is united to Christ, there is a new world, the old order has gone, and a new order has already begun.
> From first to last this has been the work of God. He has reconciled us men to himself through Christ, and he has enlisted us in this service of reconciliation. What I mean is, that God was in Christ reconciling the world to himself, no longer holding men's misdeeds against them, and that he has entrusted us with the message of reconciliation (II Cor. 5. 17, NEB).

SOME SUGGESTIONS
FOR FURTHER READING

Alan Booth, *Not Only Peace*, SCM Press (1967)

F. W. Dillistone, *The Novelist and the Passion Story*, Collins (1960)

Stanley Evans, *The Church in the Back Streets*, Mowbray (1962)

H. H. Farmer, *The Word of Reconciliation*, Nisbet (1967)

P. T. Forsyth, *The Work of Christ*, Collins (1965)

K. S. Inglis, *The Churches and the Working Classes in Victorian England*, Routledge (1963)

J. Jeremias, *Jesus' Promise to the Nations*, SCM Press (1958)

L. C. Knights, *Explorations*, Penguin (1964)

John Knox, *The Church and the Reality of Christ*, Collins (1963)

E. Thompson, *The Making of the British Working Class*, Gollancz (1964)

Paul Tillich, *Love, Power and Justice*, O.U.P. (1960)

E. R. Wickham, *Church and People in an Industrial City*, Lutterworth (1957)

B. R. Wilson, *Religion in Secular Society*, C. A. Watts (1966)